*Endorsements for "Another..."*

"*Another Way to Learn?*" is an excellent primer on home-based learning. In an age where schooling and school-based learning are invariably presented by politicians and the media as the 'only way to do it', this book presents another way – and one that puts family first. Covering everything from first principles to practical suggestions about avoiding burnout, this book presents a way to 'do family' that is attractive and exciting. "*Another Way to Learn?*" has the potential to impact a new generation of home educators – and for this we are very grateful.

**—Steve and Lyn Richards**
*Educational director SWLearning, Making the Right Impression (2007)*

With home education on the rise throughout the UK, "*Another Way to Learn?*" is an important book for our time. Molly and the team have come together to curate a wide scope of thought, experience, and advice to help equip home educators at every stage of their journey. In this book you'll read wisdom from veteran educators as well as hearing homegrown stories from fresh voices who are raising their children in this beautiful, freeing way. I'm sure you'll find your face, and family represented within this book; I'm also certain each chapter will help you find your way on the rich and rewarding adventure of home education.

**—Leah Boden**
*Author of Modern Miss Mason (Tyndale 2023)*

It's wonderful to hear British Home Ed voices in the pages of this book. Such a wealth of inspiration, encouragement, wisdom and practical insight for those embarking on their Home Ed journey or simply looking for fresh input along the way. We needed this!

**—Jacqui Wakelam**
*Mum Heart UK*

# ANOTHER WAY TO LEARN?

**DISCOVERING THE BEAUTY OF HOME EDUCATION - AN ESSENTIAL GUIDE**

# ANOTHER WAY TO LEARN?

## DISCOVERING THE BEAUTY OF HOME EDUCATION - AN ESSENTIAL GUIDE

COMPILED BY MOLLY ASHTON

Christian Year Publications

ISBN-13: 978 1 914273 25 4

Copyright © 2022 by Christian Year Publications
40 Beansburn, Kilmarnock, Scotland

**The opinions and thoughts expressed in this book are the views of the author/compiler and do not necessarily reflect the views of the Publisher.**

All rights reserved. No part of this publication may be reproduced, stored in a retrieval system, or transmitted in any form or by any other means – electronic, mechanical, photocopy, recording or otherwise – without prior permission of the copyright owner.

Typeset by John Ritchie Ltd., Kilmarnock
Printed by Bell & Bain Ltd., Glasgow

To all home educating parents past, present and future; may God bless the works of your hands as you bravely and beautifully build up the foundations of the next generation.

## *Acknowledgments*

Our thanks go to Alison Banks and Kyria Banks at John Ritchie, publishers, for their patience, creativity and willingness to work with so many of us. To Frances Robinson for her meticulous first edit, encouragement and discernment. To Andy Nicholson for his time and skills in creating our wonderful website. To Steve Beegoo for his solid support and wisdom throughout. To all our families for being their unique and colourful selves.

# *Contents*

Foreword — 1
Steve Beegoo, Head of Education at Christian Concern

Introduction: Catching a vision for family living and learning — 3
Molly Ashton

## Part 1: Finding freedom to follow a unique path — 17

1. The early years: Building good foundations — 19
   Jessica Girard

2. Exploring delight-led learning in the teen years — 41
   Dr Kat Patrick

3. Socially speaking: Understanding the home-educated child as a social being — 55
   Juliet English

4. But where will the whiteboard go?! Moving from school education to home education — 63
   Siân Lowe

5. Additional needs: Making room for disabilities, disorders, difficulties and differences — 75
   Anne Laure Jackson

## Part 2: Firm foundations through the generations — 85

6. Home education: Is it for dads too? — 87
   Charles and Ruth Barber

7. Help! My grandchildren are being home-educated: Home education and the wider family — 103
   Helen Brunning

8. Standing on the shoulders of giants: The view from second-generation home educators — 115
   Philippa Nicholson

## Part 3: Survival mode: tips and tools to see it through — 127

9. Making it work: Overcoming challenges, complications and curveballs — 129

   Part 1 - When everything is stacked against you — 129
   Kirsteen McLeod

   Part 2 - A working mum and a home-educating dad — 137
   Matthew Harris

   Part 3 - The struggle to juggle — 142
   Afia Bayayi

10. Self-care matters: Ten ways to look after yourself and avoid burnout — 147
    Catherine Shelton

11. Seeking green pastures and still waters: Why soul care is necessary for home educators — 159
    Alberta Stevens

**Conclusion: Upholding the vision** 171
Molly Ashton

**Afterword: "No! These are *our* sons and daughters."** 179
Randall and Mary Hardy

**Appendix A: Educational philosophies** 187
Juliet English

**Appendix B: Practical advice on running a home education support group** 195
Juliet English

**Appendix C: Helpful Resources** 201

**Author Biographies** 205

**Bibliography** 211

## *Foreword*

Steve Beegoo
Head of Education at Christian Concern

Home education. The very phrase may excite you, daunt you, or simply remind you of certain people in your own life – for good or ill! But if you've picked up this book, something of the importance of teaching has clearly caught your heart.

More and more, I am encountering people who are hearing the call of God to home-educate their children. More and more, I am hearing of parents being profoundly disturbed by the changes in our culture and schools. More and more, in my work, I am supporting those investigating 'Another Way To Learn'.

For Christian parents especially, the teaching of Jesus is clear, "Let the little children come to me, and do not hinder them" (Matthew 19:14). He wanted children to be taught to come to Him. He didn't want them hindered by other agendas. What will your response be to this?

This book has chapter after glorious chapter for those who are feeling drawn to take home education seriously. Read it and you will find stories, examples and advice which will guide your way, not only in thinking about your child's education, but also in your own journey of faith. And though it is written by Christians, the vulnerable, personal testimonies, combined with wise, professional and skilfully explained advice, should appeal to all readers, addressing all the key aspects prospective (and active!) home educators should be considering.

Far from becoming the isolated, anti-social young men and women society fear from the home educated, my experience is that done well, and with God at the head, home education results in community-loving, well socialised and faith-filled disciples.

It is not easy. There will be sacrifices. People will misunderstand. Those from whom you hope and expect support may criticise or disapprove. Sorry about that! But if you think that your Lord is calling, explore this book and be prepared for an adventure. Your children are worth it. And as with many aspects of the Christian life, there is so much wonderful hidden treasure to discover along the way.

Watchman Nee said, "The Christian experience, from start to finish, is a journey of faith" (2006, p.161). Never more so than in parenting. This 'journey of faith', as we consider our children, requires becoming increasingly "sure of what we hope for and certain of what we do not see" (Hebrews 11:1). For Christian parents, our faith-filled and faithful response to God's call will result in our own faith growing and, in turn, faith being sown in the hearts of our children.

So, home education? To be honest, you are already educating your children at home, more than you probably know. The only question is: what focus and form will it take, in what the Lord is leading you and your family into? Read on, and discover!

## INTRODUCTION

# CATCHING A VISION FOR FAMILY LEARNING AND LIVING

*Molly Ashton*

I am writing the start of this book from a place which holds many memories of my husband's and my home-educating years, The Bishop's Palace in Wells, Somerset. It's April, and despite the somewhat chilly gusts of wind, life is bursting forth from every corner of this beautiful garden. There is a bank of delicate yellow primroses, an arboretum floor canopied with the bright blue and yellow of crocuses and daffodils, the fresh green of new leaves, the billowy pink of a magnificent magnolia and some exuberant birdsong filling the air. There is also a steady stream of mothers and small children enjoying the fresh air and space. It doesn't seem too long ago when I was such a mum and, to be honest, I still sometimes pine for those days. In this place our children have run and played while I've sat and read. We've had many a picnic or frothy coffee with friends, we've studied trees, watched outdoor theatre and discovered local history. The children have made cars out of piles of fallen leaves and climbed 'their' special tree.

Communication with our children has been a consistent thread running through these years; one continuous conversation which lasts a lifetime (see also *axis.org*). I wonder – would I be having the deep and significant conversations with our young adult sons that I am having now, if I hadn't shared numerous earlier conversations about centipedes, Lego creations and the thousand-and-one other minutiae which are of great importance to a small boy?

So, I begin this home education manual with this message uppermost in my mind: that home education is about so much more than the successful acquisition of knowledge. Of course, it includes all the traditional aspects of learning – reading, writing, arithmetic, study of a wonderful array of subjects and the acquisition of certain skill sets. But it's also about exploring the beautiful world in which we live, snuggling up with a hot chocolate and becoming immersed in a great story-book; wondering at great inventions or breathtaking art – doing life together. It's about giving our children a real childhood and preparing them to live well as adults – all within the ups and downs of family life. And centrally, it is about the building of relationships; with God, within the family and with those around us in our community. It truly is education without walls.

I wonder why you are reading this book. Maybe you're at the beginning of your home education journey. Maybe you're well established, revelling in the freedom and fun you are having with your children. Maybe you've been walking the home education road a while and are weary and worn down by its daily challenges. Maybe you are just considering home education for your family. It's our hope and prayer that as you read this book, packed full of practical advice from experienced home educators, you will find fresh inspiration and encouragement to equip and empower you as you work out your own unique pathway along this exciting journey.

## An awakening to home education

My awakening to the fascinating and joy-filled world of home education began before marriage and children, as I got to know a family who 'home-schooled' their four children. While my first question was, "Why do that, when there's a perfectly good school down the road?", I was intrigued by several things: by the way learning was a thread woven through everyday life, by the confidence and friendliness of the children and, above all, by their evidently strong sense of family. Learning seemed to be such a natural extension of parenting. They were also one of the most hospitable families I had ever known, sharing meals, adventures, their home and their lives with many others, including my younger self. Having lived closely alongside them, the concern that home education would lead to shy children unable to relate to others was stopped before it began. On the contrary, I observed that being securely rooted in a loving family and real community resulted in happy children, able to respond well to both the sorrows and the joys in those around them.

So, the tiny seed of a vision was planted in my heart, which then lay dormant for some years. However, even back then, over twenty years ago, I found myself drawn to ponder the original design and purpose for the family; to uncover its foundations, in order to build on them afresh. For me, as a Christian, this meant digging into the Bible to discover God's intention for family life. What I found there is so appealing, and makes so much sense, that I would commend it to everyone, whatever your faith base.

## A vision for home education

Most, though tragically not all, babies begin the first few months of their lives cocooned within the warmth and safety of a loving family, with increasing forays into the wider world where their senses must tingle and their souls be excited by all they encounter. I think we would all agree that this is the best beginning for such little ones. I wonder, then: why are we so quick to push them out of this supremely nurturing environment and into nurseries, playschools and schools? It might be counter-cultural, but could we dare to believe that our children would not only develop normally, but indeed blossom and thrive if they stayed within a family environment for longer?

What if our homes continue to be places where life lessons are learnt, where the ability to relate to others is modelled, where forgiveness is freely given and received and where love for each other covers a multitude of wrongs? What if they are places where our children and others can come to find refuge from the storms of life, be restored and head out again? What if they are places where streams of living water flow, to quench thirsty souls? What if they are places where the search for knowledge is accompanied by rigorous debate so that true wisdom is gained? What if they could be places filled with laughter, music, feasting and celebration? What if they could be places where our children continue to play imaginatively, explore energetically, create messily and sleep peacefully?

What if, instead of relative strangers, we parents are the ones cleaning grazed knees, sharing a good book and teaching everyday life skills? Could we have the satisfaction of overseeing tentative steps in reading, and watching a child's face light up with sudden understanding of a mathematical concept? Could we be the ones exploring new places alongside them and learning new skills with them?

This comes with much sacrifice; it is not for the faint-hearted, and there are many hurdles along the way. However, I truly believe that when we as parents take back the central place in our children's upbringing and education – when we wholeheartedly embrace the responsibility to shape their hearts, minds and spirits – we will indeed raise strong young people confident in their unique abilities, skills and callings, ready not only to weather the storms of life but to lead others through them too.

**Threading the story of home education in Britain**

Educating our children within the family and local community is not a new concept, though it is a concept which has come under sustained pressure and attack in recent decades, from a cacophony of other voices and demands in wider society. Nevertheless, its roots can be traced back through history in just about all cultures. The Jewish people were given their mandate way back in the time of Moses to teach their children as they went about their everyday business, as they walked and talked and ate meals together. I love this model of life learning, which has been one of our family's inspirations.

# INTRODUCTION

In the UK, prior to free universal primary education, the teaching of young children predominantly took place within the home, mostly by the mother. One of my favourite heroines of the past is Susannah Wesley. She had a large number of children, and despite the poverty and challenges of life in eighteenth-century Britain, diligently taught not only her children, but also those of her neighbours, to read and write. When she needed some quiet, she would put her apron over her head and her family knew this was the signal to give her some space! Life must have been hard in ways we can only imagine, but she persevered, and two of her sons, John and Charles, became instrumental in a spiritual renewal of our nation, as well as much loved hymn writers.

Right up until the Education Act of 1870, the majority of children were mentored in the skills they needed for life initially within their own families, and then through apprenticeships in their communities. Those from wealthier homes were taught by tutors and governesses at home. Some were able to attend local schools, if finances permitted. William Shakespeare was one of these (his schoolhouse in Stratford-on-Avon is well worth a visit). In medieval times, formal education was predominantly the premise of the church, and took place in monasteries. Our first university, Oxford, was established as a place of learning in 1096, followed by Cambridge in 1209. Access to these was almost exclusively for the upper classes and so educational reform in the Victorian era, offering free schooling to all, must have been welcomed as a route out of poverty for many.

However, despite this, some children were still taught at home. Beatrix Potter was one of these. She was taught at home by governesses and spent hours outside, observing and revelling in nature. I wonder, would her carefully crafted and beautifully illustrated books have come into being if she had been confined to a classroom? Another gem of a poet and illustrator, Cicely Mary Barker, suffered with epilepsy and so she too was taught at home by a governess, enrolling at night school to study art when she was 13. Would her delightful and intricately detailed Flower Fairies, much loved by generations of girls, have ever been created if her childhood had been more conventional?

The Education Acts in this country have been numerous and varied but have included a clause allowing for eduction to be at school "or otherwise" to allow for families such as these to teach their children at home. Thus, we have had the legal basis for an enviable freedom for which those in other countries have to fight.

The beginnings of the modern-day home education movement can perhaps be traced back to the 1950s and a number of pioneering parents. The most well known of these was Joy Baker, a courageous and fiercely loving mother who won a legal victory to limit the powers of state intervention in respect of education into family life (Shute, 2008). Up until then, although the law allowed for education at home, this allowance was really intended for those who could afford governesses and tutors; it was expected that all other children would attend school. However, Joy felt that she could do a better job of educating her children herself. She believed that, as a mother, her word that her children were receiving an adequate education was proof enough and the authorities did not need any further evidence. Many years of communication followed between herself and the education authorities and her children were even forcibly removed from her for one night. Her battle, however, set the precedent for all families, whatever their income, to educate their children at home. Her story is documented in her book, 'Children in Chancery' (1964) – now out of print, but which contains many resonances with our current political climate. The freedoms we enjoy today have come at a cost and, as is discussed at greater length in the Afterword, cannot be take for granted. It is time once again to defend our families. It is we, as parents, who have ultimate responsibility for our children, not the state. Home education is on the front line of the battle against state intrusion into family life and the God-given mandate of parents to bring up their children according to His good ways.

Meanwhile, across the Atlantic, there were rumbles on a larger scale about the effectiveness, or not, of state education. John Holt, a teacher, began to question the strategies used in schools, which he proposed were "self-limiting and self-defeating, and destroy both character and intelligence" (1967, p.viii). He wrote prolifically on this and as educational reform failed to materialise, became a proponent for both home education and an 'unschooling' approach within this. Following on from this came John Taylor Gatto, an award-winning teacher in the 1970s. His books too caused a stir in state education. He proposed that mass schooling is not the same thing as education. "One of the surest ways to recognise real education is by the fact that it doesn't cost very much, doesn't depend on expensive toys or gadgets. The experiences that produce it and the self awareness that propels it are nearly free" (1992, p.70). Food for thought indeed. My copy of his book, 'Dumbing Us Down', picked up carelessly in a second-hand bookshop, is full of underlinings as I have discovered one thought-provoking gem after another.

While my mind was challenged and my preconceived thoughts rocked by the writings of these two men, my spirit was stirred, my own convictions were validated and my emerging vision began to soar when I stumbled across Clay and Sally Clarkson. With four adult children all living vibrant Christian lives, an international speaking ministry and a small library of published books to their name, they have been both pioneers and mentors to many Christian parents in the last few decades. The vision they set out for a life-giving home, based on and filled with the truth, beauty and goodness of God, has inspired countless families. Their perception and wisdom stem from a Christian foundation, but I think many of the principles they share should resonate with us all.

By the 1980s, home education had shifted from the fringes to the mainstream in the States. At the same time, the family unit was disintegrating at an unprecedented rate, as pressure upon families rose and parents increasingly delegated their central role in their children's lives to others. From their background of a ministry in Christian mission and discipleship, the Clarksons began reading about home education with respect to their own children. They quickly saw the connection between discipleship and home education and became convinced that this was the best way forward for their own family. They wrote 'Educating the Wholehearted Child' (1994) as a manual not only for educating children at home, but for discipling them within the family. Their conviction several decades ago that "Christian homeschooling is a movement of God's Spirit to restore and strengthen the family" (revised edition, 2011, p.43) was, I believe, prophetic and is even more relevant today than it was then.

**Counting the Cost**

Even once my husband and I were convinced that home education was the right way forward for our family, we had questions – not least about the financial practicalities. For us, this meant my husband becoming the sole breadwinner, something which we had not planned and which has weighed on him at times. This is certainly not the only way of working family finances, and I recommend that you turn to chapter 9 for some inspirational stories in this area.

Another concern was how we would be involved in our local community, especially since in our small rural town, the primary school is quite central to this. We decided that we would simply have to work harder at making friendships, and as life has unfolded I've been wonderfully amazed at how our ability to be 'salt and light' to others (an exhortation of Jesus to His disciples, Matthew 5:13-16) has actually been enriched by our decision to home-educate. From the beginning, our home (not the school) became central to our relationships. We invited friends home for tea and cake, for meals and for parties. We have an annual mulled wine and mince pie get-together around Christmas time, and our friends' children who twenty years ago stayed home with babysitters now turn up on their return from university. We have certainly had to be intentional about being a part of our community, but being based at home has been such a blessing to us, and I hope to others also.

**Cornerstones of home education**

So, where do we start? I have found that having a deep, unshakable conviction that home education is our calling has been essential and has carried us through the tough days and seasons. As my husband and I seek to plough our own furrow, we are not always met with genuine curiosity and open-mindedness from others. We need to be prepared for this. In addition, the day-to-day challenges can sometimes seem overwhelming and without ready support at hand, our own steadfastness can be severely tested. I would commend to you the Afterword of this book which charts the political landscape in relation to both family and education over the last few decades. This knowledge and understanding fuels my determination to keep going when the terrain is rough.

Another cornerstone is the worldview with which we approach life, and how we apply this to the parenting and teaching of our children. For some this will be faith-based, and for others it will revolve around certain values and philosophies. Education is not neutral and the foundation from which we approach it will naturally saturate our teaching of every subject. At the present time, our state education mainly stems from a humanist/Marxist philosophy (Rose, 2016). As Christian parents, we strive for our children to be taught right from the start from a biblical foundation: that they are created by God, in His image, loved unconditionally, able to receive forgiveness when they mess up, and have a mission in life which only they, with their unique gifts and character, can fulfil. In a world where so many young people are without hope, this is good news indeed. If we have the opportunity of pouring the depth and fullness of these wonderful truths into every aspect of their education, it would be hard to settle for anything less.

While this is a book about home education, I do want to mention the small but growing number of independent Christian schools across the nation which also seek to provide this biblical education. Back in the late 1990s when I met my first home-educating family, I also came across one such school, started by a group of parents and teachers from our church. Their passion for providing a faith-based, nurturing education for their children was impressive. One couple I knew moved away, but such was their conviction of the importance of Christian education that they became involved in supporting another similar school, even after their own children had grown up. I know of several schools which offer places for home-educated students one day a week. I personally would love to see collaboration like this continuing as we share a joint purpose to bring up our children in God's ways. There is a link in the glossary for The Christian Schools Trust if this is something you would like to explore further.

Once we've thought about our foundations, we might like to look at our ideas about learning, what we think constitutes education and how that happens. Appendix 1 on educational philosophies explains this a little further. It can be helpful to observe our children's learning styles; visual, auditory or kinaesthetic. We can make the most of their individual interests and passions and use these as a base for a delight-filled variety of learning activities (Bogart, 2019). We can look at our children's unique skills and abilities and think how we might nurture these. From when our children were a very young age, I've prayed that I would be able to recognise their most significant abilities, know how to encourage them, and bring others alongside to do so where we as parents can't. Time and again I've seen these prayers answered.

I find that having a long-term view reduces the pressure on me significantly and enables us all to enjoy the journey of learning and living. As Mary Hood (1994, p.18) asks, "When you look at your own children and picture them at age eighteen, what do you hope to see?"

Character development is not something which is on most school curricula, or even included in many parenting courses, but I would suggest that this too is at the heart of what we do as home-educating parents. The introduction to Dietrich Bonhoeffer's life in 'The Cost of Discipleship' (1937) describes his character first, leaving his considerable academic achievements until later: "From his father, Dietrich Bonhoeffer inherited goodness, fairness, self-control and ability; from his mother, his great human understanding and sympathy, his devotion to the cause of the oppressed, and his unshakeable steadfastness" (p.11). Strength of character is what keeps us standing when all around us seems to be collapsing; it's what enables our children to think independently and then act according to conscience, rather than following the crowd; it's where the self-discipline comes from to study hard for a degree or get up in the dark each morning to go to work. Virtuous characters don't grow overnight, but by painstakingly and patiently teaching our children good ways to act and react to circumstances and people.

And finally, and probably the most fun of these starting points, is to dream! What are your ideals? How would you like your family to look? What would you consider to be a delight and curiosity-led education? How do you and your children like spending your days? What kind of memories do you want to create for them? Allow your dreams to meander down a myriad of lanes.

None of the above points are one-off activities. Even as one who has been home-educating for years, I find it helpful to revisit all these concepts periodically and re-apply them to our growing and changing family.

**Practical tips**

Now for some tangible tips to tick off on a 'to-do' list. Subsequent chapters are packed full of practical advice, so this is only a very scant overview, with suggestions collated from home-educating families old and new. While this might be most helpful to those at the beginning of the journey, I hope there might also be a couple of nuggets useful to more established home educators.

Collating a good collection of books is a great joy and will pay dividends in years to come. You may be a bookworm already, but even so, I'm sure our homes can never become too full of books as our interests and children grow. I love rooting around second-hand bookshops, charity shops or garage sales, or searching online to find specific books, both old and new. Become a second-hand book squirrel. I would also recommend making library visits part of your regular routine. Our children have enjoyed a wide selection of books, including ones which Victorian educator and home-education pioneer Charlotte Mason would call 'twaddle' (1886, p.205). However, I do try to steer them towards books which are well written, as this is a wonderful way of imbibing rich language and great concepts, as well as firing their imagination (Schaeffer Macaulay, 1984). I am also a fan of using picture books well beyond the toddler years. One of the great advantages of a picture book is that the whole story can be read in one sitting. Another is that a well-illustrated book can be for a child like having an art gallery in his or her lap (Mackenzie, 2018). I also find that the combination of pictures and text can both reinforce and soften difficult topics.

Books are also a good way of teaching our children the difference between good and evil, right and wrong. Older classics such as 'The Lord of the Rings' contain an obvious clash of worldviews, but I have found that many, though not all, more recent books blur traditional ideas of right and wrong. For younger children, I'm convinced a truth-based foundation is the best beginning. From this, they can learn to discern as they get older. Bank tellers are taught to identify false bank notes by handling hundreds of true ones, and I have found this concept to be helpful in guiding my choice of books, audibles, movies and music. This has been easier with our older children than our younger ones, as in the intervening years technology has become more and more entrenched in daily life. While this has had many advantages, ease of access alongside a lowering of the moral bar of content can leave me feeling like I'm trying to stem the flow of a mighty dyke with my little finger! I've regretted the times I have not been vigilant about their media exposure, as what feeds their minds and imaginations really does impact their emotions and thus their hearts and behaviour. This is a challenge to us as parents that no previous generation has known and I'm grateful for friends with whom I can share it.

A second foray could be to amass some basic equipment. There are so many tempting resources on the market, but most are unnecessary and expensive. Nevertheless, I have also learnt that in some things it may be a false economy to buy cut-price bargains, and that our children will be better inspired and inclined to enjoy a subject or try a new skill with good quality tools (Levison, 2000). We applied this principle when we bought our eldest son's viola, and it not only spared our ears, but I'm sure also contributed to his love and perseverance in learning this instrument as he took pleasure in the sounds he made.

Creating space to store the increasing library of books and all the equipment and clutter that is part and parcel of home education can be a challenge. For those of you who are well established, I wonder if the way you use space has changed over the years? It has for us; some ideas I've picked up along the way have led to us establishing a nature table, a craft cupboard, an artist box, a classical composer shelf, a box for sports equipment, space for science projects, a poetry tea shelf and also their own patch in the garden (though this periodically is taken over by me and my vegetables!).

**Never stop learning**

I am a dreamer and an idealist. I've had to learn in my own mothering journey to accept the messes, the brokenness, the fractured relationships and the everyday challenges, and learn that these too, by some amazing miracle, can become part of the beauty and wholeness of each of us. But my dream for family only burns more and more deeply in my heart as we weather each storm, and also as I look around at the confusion and pain so many other children in our nation are suffering. That breaks my heart and should be cause enough for each of us to question how we can do better for our own children.

So, as we draw to a close here, what are your thoughts? What is stirring in your heart? What do you yearn for, for your family? Dream a little ... and then read on! I commend to you every chapter of this book, written by home educators across the UK; some of them veterans with a depth of experience and the long view, and some newer, with a fresh approach to what the first tentative steps of home education might look like. We have divided the book into three parts: initially focussing on the child's learning, then spanning out to some issues for us as parents, and finally zooming out to look at how home education impacts the wider family.

We never stop learning ourselves, and even after all these years I've found welcome advice and wisdom as I've read each chapter. Above all I've found encouragement; home-educating parents in the UK are not alone, but part of a growing movement, gaining in numbers and passion.

Happy reading, friend and fellow traveller. May your dreams be extravagant, your courage great and your celebrations joyous as you seek to restore the heart and true purpose of the family to our nation.

PART 1

# FINDING FREEDOM TO FOLLOW A UNIQUE PATH

CHAPTER ONE

# THE EARLY YEARS: BUILDING GOOD FOUNDATIONS

*Jessica Girard*

It was a gloriously sunny day at the end of summer when I walked my recently turned 4-year-old down the hill to the nearby parish school. She looked adorable in her grey pleated pinafore dress paired with frilly white socks that were tucked into the cutest black patent T-bar buckle shoes – the kind that are only made for little girls. She still had that toddler-like chub about her cheeks and her soft blonde hair was tied neatly behind her head, as per school policy. As we walked down the hill, hand in hand, she carried on her back an oversized red backpack filled with a lunchbox, a snack pot, a water bottle, her PE kit and a spare pair of knickers (one must always be prepared). She reminded me of a little pack donkey; it was a cute but comical sight to behold.

After a five-minute walk, we passed the row of horse chestnut trees that lead to the black iron school gates. The trees would soon be dropping their seeds and I felt a tinge of sadness that we wouldn't have as much freedom to collect autumn treasures this year as we had done in the years before. We bustled our way through the growing crowd of parents and children all saying their farewells and tucking in shirts that were already coming loose, to reach the back of the old Victorian school building where the reception children were to be deposited. Here I handed over my firstborn child to a kindly teacher, whom I'd met only twice previously and had just one conversation with.

Both my daughter and I were holding it together pretty well in comparison to other families around us. I was calm and composed in that stoic, stiff-upper-lip British way, determined not to shed a tear in front of her, nor cause a scene in public. She was excited about her first day, quietly confident as she so often is, and happily stomped off into her new classroom showing no sign of pining for her dear mother. My little pack donkey was all grown up.

Childless in the playground, I was doing pretty well – that is, until I opened the little goody bag that had been handed to me by the teacher in exchange for my daughter. I saved the bag to open at work, shedding only a few quiet tears as I strolled back. Once at my desk, I opened the bag, which contained a tissue, a teabag, a chocolate and a little poem. The poem broke me:

> *"The day is finally here and now you are alone,*
> *Sit down to have a brew and think of how they've grown!*
> *The tissue is for you to have a little cry,*
> *And now they are at school, remember times gone by.*
> *As you eat your treat your worries can be gone,*
> *We already love your precious little one!"*

Thankfully, I share an office with just one other colleague, for I was now sobbing at my desk, a full-on 'ugly cry'. My wise, patient colleague, a mother with far more years of experience than myself, took the poem from my hand, read it, rolled her eyes and tossed it into the rubbish bin in the corner. It turns out that one tissue really isn't enough if you're going to point out to a bereft mother how alone she now is. Needless to say, the one chocolate, as yummy as it was,

was also woefully insufficient to meet my comfort-eating needs – I needed at least ten more to hit that sweet spot.

What was intended as a sweet gesture of reassurance from the school turned out not only to be a tad insensitive, but also to be the catalyst for me to pursue home-educating my daughter. For, you see, I was not ready for the good times to be gone – especially not after just four short years. But it was the final line of the poem that sealed it for me: that declaration of love for my child – a child the teacher had only spent five minutes alone with prior to this first day of school. No, they barely knew my child, and they certainly didn't love her.

It was then that I had an epiphany of sorts, an 'Aha!' moment that filled me with good old-fashioned gumption and washed away all the doubts that had clouded my mind in recent years whenever my husband and I had considered home education.
No-one knows my daughter like I do.
No-one loves my daughter like I do.
No-one is better placed to educate my daughter than I am.

It was a powerful, affirming moment, and by the end of that first school week we were ready to move forward with home educating.

**The 'why' before the 'how'**

Since we started home educating my eldest daughter a few years ago, I have met with a number of families to discuss the possibility of their doing the same, as well as countless others who have reached out online. They usually start by asking me what we do and are then very eager to know how we do it. This line of thought often gets people bogged down in the 'how to' of home educating before they have given much thought as to the 'why'.

Personally, I feel it's important to understand *why* you want to home-educate your children before you start planning *how* to go about it. By clarifying your vision and pinpointing your educational values first, before you get bogged down in curriculum choices and group signups, you will save yourself a lot of time and effort. It makes much more sense to plan your child's education once you have a clear picture of the sort of education you are wanting to provide.

Now for some, home educating is thrust upon them due to life circumstances, such as a lack of local school options, issues with bullies, the child's educational needs not being met, or issues with mental health. For these parents, the decision to withdraw a child from school and educate at home is not necessarily a choice they want to make, but it is a choice that feels right for their child. Often, in time, they come to love the change in educational approach, once they see the positive impact it is having on their child.

However, for many families, particularly those with young children, home educating is fast becoming their number one educational choice – something they want to embark on right from the start.

For me, despite briefly enrolling my daughter in the local school, home education was always my first choice. I had spent years researching educational philosophies and following home-school blogs right back when my eldest was still just a newborn. This is partly why I felt able to jump into action and withdraw my daughter so quickly from the school – I already knew my 'why'.

So, what drew me to want to home-educate my young children and what draws other parents to do likewise? Well, there are a number of factors that come into play, some religious, some cultural, some purely practical.

I often joke when people ask me why I home-educate that it's because I'm too lazy for the school run! That's partly true, because I don't like to be rushed and nor does my youngest daughter, so our slow starts to the day have been a blessing to us both; but honestly, the freedom and flexibility of our day without the constraints of the school timetable has contributed to a much slower pace of life for us, which is definitely part of my 'why'.

There's also no denying that home educating allows you to live out your family values in a more focused way, embedding them into your family culture. As a Christian, I've been able to add Scripture and prayers to our days with much more ease than many of my friends who find 'Bible time' to be a sporadic add-on to the end of their child's day. I didn't choose to home-educate for religious purposes, feeling the school environment would be a bad moral influence (as some do), but I have come to love how my children and I can linger over our devotions in the morning. We take time to discuss and unpack Scripture together, sing hymns aloud together and encourage one another in prayer. It's become a special time and affirming for me to see them exploring and growing in their own journey of faith.

So, religious and cultural aspects do make up part of the 'why' for many, as you can incorporate the things that are most important to your family, things that just wouldn't be prioritised, or often respected, in schools.

When speaking with other families though, I've come to notice a recurring theme that is drawing many to home-educate, and that is the desire to provide their children with an unhurried childhood. It's very much a lifestyle choice in many ways, which I believe can be summed up in what Charlotte Mason, the Victorian educational reformist, called "a quiet growing time" (1886, p.43, see also Appendix A).

In the first volume of her home education series, Charlotte said, "In this time of extraordinary pressure, educational and social, perhaps a mother's first duty to her children is to secure for them a quiet growing time, a full six years of passive receptive life" (ibid.).

Interestingly, even back in the early 1900s parents appear to have been under "extraordinary pressure" when it came to educating their children, and I can't help but think it has only got worse. This pressure is becoming more and more unwelcome amongst parents and children alike and, as more research is coming out about the benefits of delayed academics for children, as well as more awareness about different educational approaches (such as those of Steiner, Reggio and Montessori), more and more parents are beginning to feel that sense of 'duty' that Charlotte spoke about.

The most common school starting age worldwide is now 6 years old, which lines up with Charlotte's recommendation, but here in the UK we send our children to school at just 4 years old, where they are swiftly being taught to read and write, even if they lack the attention and ability to yet master it.

More and more parents that I speak with are simply uncomfortable with this approach in education and would prefer for the school starting age to be raised in line with the rest of the world. Many even consider delaying their child's school entry but soon learn that to do so the child would have to skip a year or two and enter the school system in Year 1 or 2, raising concerns that their child would be educationally behind their peers. Unfortunately, the school system in the UK is not as flexible as in many other countries – classrooms are rigidly organised by age rather than ability.

The good thing is that parents these days seem to be much more aware of their rights and less inclined to put up with a system they're not happy with. Although most who come to home-educate their children in the early years know nothing of Charlotte Mason's inspirational educational reforms, I am finding that many are desiring for their children exactly what Charlotte was advocating, that 'passive receptive life' where their children can be young and carefree for as long as possible – free to play unhindered and learn unencumbered by the pressures of the school system.

I think for many parents, myself included, when it comes to educating our children, we find ourselves asking, "Surely there is another way?" A way for our children to learn with freedom and joy, a way that respects them as the individuals that they are with unique personalities, interests and giftings, and a way that honours their childhood as not just something to be rushed through. As Tom Stoppard said, just "because children grow up, we think a child's purpose is to grow up. A child's purpose is to be a child" (2014, p.83). More and more parents are wanting to secure this kind of protected childhood for their children.

That protection of childhood, along with letting my kids be little for as long as possible, was what really drew me to home-educate in the first place and makes up a large portion of my 'why'. I challenge you to take some time to think of your own 'why' and to really pinpoint the values you hold that you want to see come to fruition through home educating.

Perhaps ask yourself:

- Why does home educating feel like a good idea for my family?
- What educational philosophies draw me and why?
- How would home educating benefit my children?
- What values could we practise more easily though home educating?
- What are my child's unique talents and interests? How can these be best encouraged?
- What do I want the atmosphere of our home to look like?
- What sort of learning environment do I want to create for my children?
- How do I want my child to describe his home education/childhood?
- What is my greatest wish for my children?

Once your 'why' is clear in your mind, and you know what your education values are and the atmosphere of learning you are trying to create, you can then move on to how to achieve that practically. By staying rooted in your 'why' you'll be better able to avoid decision fatigue and feel more confident in your own planning, able to veto curricula, resources, groups and even subjects that, although very good and life-giving to some, just don't align with the educational values and atmosphere you are trying to create in your home school.

**Practical tips for home-educating young children**

Now the beauty of home-educating younger children is that there is less academic pressure as you begin. You have much more freedom to play and follow individual interests, particularly in those early years of education, before you slowly start to introduce more formal, academic learning.

My advice to new home educators is always to start small – get one plate spinning before you start to spin the next. This can be harder to do for those withdrawing a child from the school system as the child has become used to a structured learning timetable; the parents often feel pressured to try and recreate school at home and provide them with the same level of vigour. You have to remember, though, that the purpose of home educating is not to recreate school at home! Far from it. By home educating you will have the freedom and flexibility to provide your child with a variety of creative learning opportunities that just can't be achieved within the school system.

For those withdrawing a child from school, there will inevitably be a transition period. The advice often cited to parents withdrawing their children from school is to allow for a period of 'de-schooling' that will enable your child to decompress and process the changes that are happening. This is easier to do with younger children as they won't have clocked up as many years in the system, so will need less time to adjust to their new normal, plus they're often happier to be freer in their play and exploration. Consider it to be a prolonged summer holiday period, when the child can enjoy various activities and outings, along with lots of free play and time outdoors, before you start to slowly introduce the academic subjects that are appropriate for their age and stage. How long to de-school is up to you, but a month of de-schooling for every year that your child has been in school is often recommended. You may prefer to allocate just one school term for the transition, or even one academic year, depending on how your child has been affected by the school system. Be guided by their needs, adding in lessons if they're ready or extending the transition period if they're proving reluctant at first. By the time your de-schooling is over, you will have both learnt how to separate learning from school, thus enabling you to be freer and more flexible in your home learning styles.

After withdrawing my daughter from school, my main focus for her first term of home education was simply to establish a good daily and weekly rhythm that would serve us well for many years to come. Ideas for this rhythm are covered later in this chapter. Once it was established and that metaphorical plate was spinning well, I then introduced nature study to our week, the only subject I included in our curriculum before she turned 6 years old. This mostly involved lots of time outdoors getting up close to nature, coupled with some great seasonal reading aloud. It secured that quiet growing time that I was after, leaving her with lots of time to play with her younger sister and develop at her own speed.

Now whether it be an 8-year-old who is being withdrawn from school or a 4-year-old who is starting home education right from the beginning, my advice to parents is always the same: keep it simple and start slow.

## Keep it simple

Kim John Payne highlighted the negative effects of 'too much, too fast, too soon' in his powerful book 'Simplicity Parenting: Using the Extraordinary Power of Less to Raise Calmer, Happier and More Secure Kids' (2009); I'd highly recommend reading it. As you start out on your home education journey with your precious little ones, you want to ensure that you don't pursue too much, too fast, too soon and risk being overwhelmed and burning out.

This simplified approach to education in the early years, particularly as we as parents and home educators transition into the lifestyle and find our feet, often requires that we keep ourselves in check when we feel the societal, cultural and familial pressure to prove ourselves. It's essential that we keep our child's best interests central. Keeping it simple and starting slowly is, more often than not, in the best interests of younger children, especially those who are starting out in home education – so let no-one sway you otherwise.

*1. Be guided by your 'why'*

As mentioned earlier, once you have established the reasons why you want to home-educate, hold that vision and those values close to mind. That way, as you navigate the journey ahead, inevitably hitting a few roadblocks along the way, you'll remember why you started out on this journey and can be guided by your educational values as you move forward.

When I started home educating, with a 4 and 3-year-old in the home, I typed up my vision and values for the early years of education and put it on display on the kitchen noticeboard. It served as a constant reminder to me as to why I was doing what I was doing and what I was trying to achieve for my girls. So, write down your 'why'. It can be in your journal or your planning folder or maybe on display like mine. Regularly refer back to it as you decide what resources you want to invest in, what groups you want to sign up to and how you want to implement certain subjects.

Keeping my 'why' close has given me the confidence to turn down groups and pass on curricula that on the surface all offered great learning experiences, but deep down conflicted with our value of a calm, unhurried home education schedule which provides space for lots of free play and family time.

## 2. Prioritise relationships over academics

One of the best things about home educating is the additional time we get with our children. It can feel like both a blessing and a curse at times, but it really is a privilege to share in so much of their childhood and education.

There will of course be days, particularly when home-educating little ones, when squabbles will happen, attitudes will stink, frustrations will rise and explosions will happen (more often than not, by you!). I know this to be the case in my home. That idyllic vision of home educating doesn't always quite match up with reality and it's on those days when sibling tensions are rising and my patience is waning, when I've snapped and feelings are hurt, that I've learnt to put down the books, push away the maths and do something to reconnect as a family. The lessons can wait, your relationships cannot. Plus, we all learn best with happy hearts and calm minds, so don't be afraid to stop mid-lesson to avert a fallout when frustrations are rising. You can simply return to it another day.

## 3. Start and end the day right

Simple practices at the start and end of the day can make your school day run much more smoothly. To start the day right in our home we dress and make our beds before breakfast, so that following breakfast we can move straight onto our chores and schoolwork. Now some families are happy to do school in their PJs most days, but for us, getting dressed first thing ensures we have no late-morning dressing battles when we're already running late for a group and it allows me to be more fun and spontaneous with our learning, taking things outdoors when the weather allows.

I've come to learn, though, that one of the best ways to start the day right is actually by ending the previous day right. A quick 30-minute prep at the end of each day allows me to tidy up our learning spaces, pre-read the maths lesson and lay out the books needed for the next day. This simple practice means that I am better prepared for our school day, aware of what goals I'm trying to achieve and better able to direct my girls and avoid my own procrastination.

You may like to start the day with prayer and journalling and end it with lunch prep for the next day. Whatever the practices look like for you, they should help you to prepare mentally and physically for the school day ahead, enabling you to teach from a place of rest and positivity.

### *4. Create margin in your days*

When it comes to home educating younger children, you are going to need to add a lot of margin to your day – even more so if you're home educating with babies, toddlers and pre-schoolers in tow. We have a toddler in the house, and I can tell you from experience that most days you will not tick off everything on your to-do list; there will always be something unexpected that crops up and it's best to allow margin in your day to deal with this.

There are days when the maths lesson gets interrupted by a much-needed nappy change or the history lesson gets pushed back to cuddle and calm down an overloaded pre-schooler. Likewise, there could be teething babies, poorly puppies, unexpected visitors, last-minute appointments and 6-year-old divas who are just having a bad Wednesday. Sometimes it's you having the bad Wednesday!

My advice as someone who has walked this road is simply to lighten the load, keep your to-do list short and add in some much-needed margin to your day. That way you will be less hurried and better able to adjust and catch up when things don't go to plan.

*5. Replenish your soul*

According to Sarah Mackenzie in her excellent book, 'Teaching from Rest', "How you teach is just as important as what you teach" (2015, p.23), and I have to say I completely agree. When many of us turn to home education so as to avoid the stresses and pressures of an overburdened school system, we don't want to let the responsibility of home educating our children overburden us and become a cause for stress, anxiety and burnout. This sort of teaching would not be healthy for us or our children, for the old saying remains true: you cannot pour from an empty cup.

It is therefore essential that you learn to teach from a place of rest and that you prioritise your own self-care. I am by no means perfect at this and regularly return to Lisa Grace Byrne's book, 'Replenish', which has served me well for many years now. She tells us that "The road to the life we desire is the road to establishing deep anchors of wellness so we aren't so drastically tossed around when life gets stormy" (2013, p.19). When I find life getting stormy and home education feeling more stressful, that is when I realise that I'm probably slacking on my own self-care and wellness. Identifying your core essentials for wellbeing and adding in some simple, habitual self-care practices can enable you to feel calmer and better grounded as a home educator.

**Start slow**

I mentioned earlier that when I started out home-educating my 4-year-old daughter, the first thing I focused on was establishing a predictable daily rhythm that would serve our home school well for years to come.

The highly scheduled timetable of school is necessary when you have a large number of children to control and co-ordinate, but at home such a schedule is unnecessary and can take the fun, flexibility and freedom out of learning. A predictable rhythm on the other hand is not only reassuring to most children, it ensures that you also get stuff done, while being flexible and enjoyable in the process. A natural ebb and flow to the day where chores follow breakfast, maths follows chores, then a morning walk and lunch, followed by a family read-aloud and an afternoon of play. The day may start at 9am one day and 10am the next, but the flow is the same. There is no pressure, no falling behind; instead, there is flexibility to linger longer over that book you're all enjoying so much, or to skip maths today because you woke up late and need to get outdoors before the rain hits.

So, I encourage you to start slow and allow yourself time to establish a rhythm to your days before you get too bogged down in lessons. Let me share with you ten ways to add rhythm to your day, which may help guide you when establishing your own routine.

*1. Chores*

I start here on purpose. If your family is anything like mine, then by spending more time at home learning you are going to create a lot more mess. To preserve your sanity and help make time and space for enjoying this home education experience, everyone needs to muck in to help keep the learning environment at its best. Even the littlest of students can play a part in this. My girls started out with morning chores when they were both pre-schoolers by simply helping to unload the dishwasher – yes, it would have been quicker to do it myself, but now at ages 8 and 6 they are responsible for making their beds, unloading the dishwasher, unloading the washing machine and sorting the recycling in the morning, all before we start our school day.

I highly recommend tackling the bulk of the chores first thing in the morning, right after breakfast and before getting stuck in with the days formal learning. You may have heard it said, "Eat a live frog first thing in the morning and nothing worse will happen to you for the rest of the day!" In our house we 'eat our frog' by getting our chores and maths lessons out of the way first thing in the morning; the rest of the day's learning is always more welcome after that. Plus, life skills are just so important – I mean, who wants an 18-year-old that can do long division but can't even do a load of laundry? Not me! So, put them to work on the chores before you put them to work on their maths!

## 2. Table Time

Straight after breakfast and chores we move onto our 'Table Time' work. In our home, Table Time ensures that we get essential formal learning done. I started this practice once my eldest turned 6 (the equivalent of Year 2 of the school system) and was ready for more formal lessons. During Table Time I introduced the daily maths lesson, reading practice and writing. To begin with it lasted all of 20 minutes. These days, now my eldest is in the junior school years, it can last a good hour, sometimes a little longer if she's engrossed in a piece of work. This is the spot in our day that looks most like school, as I guide my daughters through their maths lessons at the table, do some reading practice with my 6-year-old, review spellings with my 8-year-old and encourage them both to do some writing.

It is also a great space to encourage independent work as your children get older. At 8 years old, my eldest daughter now works her way through a few independent tasks each day, such as reading practice, copy work, poetry and book illustrations, times-table practice, letters to pen pals and prayer or nature journalling. Even my 6-year-old now independently gets on with her copy work and illustrations.

## 3. Book basket

A morning practice, sometimes called 'circle time' or 'morning basket' is a popular choice amongst those home-educating younger children. It allows you to group lots of the smaller, often overlooked subjects together, so as to ensure that the good and beautiful things of an education aren't crowded out.

I started a book basket practice with my daughter when she was just 3 years old. It began with tales from Beatrix Potter, and a year later had grown to include our daily Bible reading, some poetry and folk tales.

Some people like to gather for their book basket first thing each day. I love this idea, but it hasn't worked for us. It doesn't really matter when you do it in your day though, what matters is that you establish a time each day that provides you with a rich learning space where you'll have the opportunity to cover a lot of lessons across multiple ages and abilities. Here is how I structure our book baskets. We cover:

- Devotions: a daily Bible reading, prayer and gratitude journal, and sometimes a biography.
- Art enrichment: daily poetry with a picture study, composer study, hymn or folk song.
- Main lesson: either nature study, history, geography or occasionally some Personal, Social, Health and Economic (PSHE) education.

*4. Mealtimes*

Mealtimes are a natural spot in the day when we gather together as a family, and are therefore a great time to tag on some extra learning opportunities. It is often said that "the fondest memories are made when gathered around the table", so make these gatherings all the more enjoyable with some light learning moments. In our home we listen to audiobooks over lunch and tag on poetry readings, book clubs and family board games to snack time. I've known of some families that actually do their entire book basket over lunch time, as they all munch away, because little ones often have a lot more attention when their hands are busy and their tummies are full. It's so simple but it works.

Often, if there is something I'm struggling to fit into our week (as was the case with board games), I look at which snack time is free and tag it on there. By adding in learning opportunities to the well-established rhythms of our day such as mealtimes, I've been able to build up our learning over time in a slow, methodical way that has been very stress-free.

## 5. Read aloud

My girls stopped napping a long time ago and my attempts at turning nap time into rest time in their rooms failed miserably, so instead I started a read-aloud time after lunch, whilst their baby brother is napping. This ensures we all get a quiet siesta in the day, which is something my introverted soul really craves, but also ensures they're quiet during their brother's nap – so it's a win-win!

Most importantly, it allows us to connect over a good book, which often acts as a pressure valve in the day, releasing any stresses or tensions from any troublesome morning interactions or tricky maths problems. The book we read at this time is not attached to any of our main lessons; it's purely for literary enjoyment. Read-aloud time has fast become one of our favourite times of the school day. I encourage you to read aloud to your children every day and not just at bedtime, for reading aloud to your children will spark their imagination, grow their vocabulary, and expand their understanding of the world.

## 6. Afternoon activities

In true Charlotte Mason home-school fashion (1886, p.23, see also Appendix A), I attempt to get all our main schoolwork out of the way before lunch, so that our afternoons can be free for the groups and learning activities that so often get crowded out of the typical school day. Things like baking and board games are wonderful for practising maths and cooperative skills, painting and handicrafts get the artistic juices flowing, and poetry teas and book clubs enable you to find joy in literature. All of these activities and more make for some fun and creative learning opportunities in our home.

We also use the afternoons to attend swimming lessons and choir practice, go for nature walks and field trips and of course dedicate lots of time for free play. You could also include music practice and sports groups here, as well as personal hobbies and household projects.

## 7. Time outdoors

I like to allow time in our day for outdoor play in nature, even if this is only in the back garden, for not only is nature calming for children, it also fuels their curiosity and creativity. As Richard Louv explains so aptly in his book, 'Last Child in the Woods' (2013), time outdoors in nature affords children the freedom to find themselves in a fantasy world, a place quite separate from the pressures of the adult world, which can only be a good thing.

Time outdoors, you see, is no add-on; it is essential for a child's learning, as well as their physical and mental health, and I'd encourage you to find space in your daily rhythm for it. Even if you don't have a garden, you could include a post-breakfast walk around the block, alternate afternoons at different parks and playgrounds through the week, or arrange playdates at nature reserves. Be intentional about it – the fresh air and physical activity will do you all the world of good.

*8. Screen time*

Screen time is definitely a tool you want in your learning arsenal, but I caution you to use it wisely and sparingly and set the boundaries of its use from the get-go. I know from experience that poor behaviour, lack of attention and sensory meltdowns tend to be a natural outflow of excessive screen use, so don't allow screens to become a distraction or a crutch in your home school.

My girls rarely watch anything now that our screen rules are well established. They know they get to watch a movie once a week and they're now content with that. As a low-tech family, we haven't yet ventured too much into the world of apps, but we do make use of short educational videos from sites like BBC Bitesize and BBC Teach during our book baskets, particularly for science and history, so that we can really bring a topic to life. We also love nature documentaries and try to make time for one or two per week, either before or after dinner. So, despite being rather low-tech in our home school, we still use screens a fair few times a week as there is no denying that they do offer some wonderful learning opportunities. It's all about making screens work for you and not against you, so that you can optimise their true educational value.

## 9. Free play

Don't underestimate the importance of free play. More and more primary schools are adding free play time into their schedules and rightly so; it's a great opportunity for children to express themselves, practise new skills and process what they've been learning in the classroom, not to mention de-stress. We scatter lots of free play opportunities throughout our home-school day; it uses up some of that much-needed margin I spoke about earlier, aids as a transition from Table Time to Book Basket, makes up a fair portion of our afternoons and ensures that the children have the time and space they need to simply be children, which is a big part of why I home-educate.

It's also worth noting that in the harder seasons of life when stress and uncertainty are greater, it's important to up the amount of free play accordingly. Not only will the extra play time aid your children's mental and emotional health in a similar way that time in nature does, but I assure you they'll be learning plenty when left to their own devices. In the months after my son was born, I hit a rough patch both physically and mentally, and our school day mostly consisted of free play interrupted by meals and read-alouds. Any guilt I had for being such a slack home educator was soon relieved when I observed the free play that overflowed from reading 'The Voyages of Dr Dolitte' to my girls. They wholeheartedly assumed the role of naturalists, researched exotic animals in our nature guides, caught bugs in the garden to observe and draw, mapped the Doctor's route to South America, wrote letters to each other in tribal symbols and narrated the story with their own toy animals – and all because they simply had the time to play.

## 10. Bedtime wind-down

Now schools may close at 3pm, but the learning never has to stop when you opt for the flexible learning lifestyle that is home education. Bedtime, like mealtimes, is another fixed point in the day that is perfect for adding in some rich learning opportunities that will also help wind your young children down for bed. Think puzzles and audiobooks – both are popular in our home, and then at bedtime itself, don't miss the opportunity for another read-aloud. In our home at bedtime, we often revisit books we've loved on previous occasions.

**Home educating with little ones in tow**

Home educating young children brings a lot of joy and I absolutely love it, but it also presents a challenge when you have even younger children in the home that also have to fit into the school day somehow. I have home-educated with a baby, a toddler and a pre-schooler in the house, and have learned that there are some simple things you can do to make things run more smoothly.

*1. Include them as much as possible*

The beauty of home educating is that you can tailor learning for multiple ages, and this can include even the youngest members of the home. My baby boy has tagged along on many a history fieldtrip, loves a nature walk as much as my girls do, and sits through lunch time audiobooks whilst he munches away. Yes, some lessons are harder to teach with him around, but we try to include him as much as possible, each taking our turn to play with and entertain him.

*2. Make use of naps*

If you have young children in the home that are still napping, then utilise these naps as much as possible. When my son was a baby, we did maths during his morning nap and book basket during his lunch-time nap. It was the only way we could get the things that required more concentration done. Even now we do most of our read-alouds during his naps, and also sometimes watch some documentaries, so that little eyes and minds aren't subjected to screens too early.

*3. Distract them with toys and/or snacks*

Activity boxes (we call them 'busy boxes') are a great idea for little ones. When my middle child was a pre-schooler, I alternated busy boxes on a daily basis so she had a variety of puzzles and activities to keep her entertained during book baskets once her attention had waned. Even now at 6 years old, she still likes to keep her hands busy with colouring or Lego, but she's still listening away. Even our toddler has various little baskets of toys that we whip out just for certain activities so that they hold their charm for longer; failing that, we appease him with a few blueberries or cheese sticks if we need to finish a piece of work.

### 4. Lower your expectations

You're raising little people and that is a full-time job, so lower your expectations a little when it comes to home educating, simplify the schedule and lighten the load. This is where allowing for margin in your day will help, particularly when educating with a baby in the home, when (for a season) the feed/nap/change/repeat schedule dominates so much of your life. During these seasons of parenting, 'survival schooling' feels a more apt name than 'home schooling', so just embrace it and extend yourself a little grace. Choose your top three priorities for the school day and be content to just get those things done. For me survival schooling with a baby in tow looked like daily writing practice, a read-aloud and some sort of afternoon activity, which some days was simply a documentary or reciting poetry.

### 5. Distraction-free times

Having times when your little ones are taken care of can be a real blessing for you and your older kids; you'll be amazed at how much work you can whizz through when not chasing the toddler! When my eldest was 5 years old, her younger sister went to a playschool group twice a week; this allowed us some time to practice phonics without interruption and read stories that would have been too long-winded for my youngest.

Utilise grandparents if you can, or arrange swaps with other home-educating friends, to allow you some distraction-free learning time to tackle the things that need more of your input.

# CHAPTER ONE

**You are your child's first teacher**

Home educating my young children is proving to be one of the greatest joys of my life. I will be forever grateful that I found the courage to follow my heart and create this lifestyle of learning I wanted to provide for my children. I often get asked how long I will home-educate them for, and my response is always, "As long as I can". I hope to go the distance – I'll see them right through to higher education if I have my way.

Yes, there are seasons of life when home educating feels hard and doubts creep in. I've walked through these seasons myself. During these times I find myself holding onto the truth that Rahima Baldwin Dancy (1989) taught me as I embarked on not just my journey of home education, but my journey of motherhood (I encourage you to hold on to it too): You are your child's first teacher. You are also their best one. You taught them to walk and you taught them to talk. You taught them how to love and how to play, and it needn't stop there, for there is no-one better equipped to love and teach your child than you.

CHAPTER TWO

# EXPLORING DELIGHT-LED LEARNING IN THE TEEN YEARS

*Dr Kat Patrick*

This chapter is about educating your older children in a way that others might think is outside of the box, but which will build their learning around their unique passions and talents. My assumption is that, as a home educator, you are accustomed to thinking (or *becoming* accustomed to thinking) outside of the box already, but sometimes – and especially when our children hit their teen years – we second-guess our creativity and fall back into the kind of schooling we're more familiar with.

We can do this even if it goes against some of our reasons for choosing to home-educate in the first place. I want to offer encouragement and some tools to help you continue with the pathways you've chosen for your own children through their teen years, because these will almost always be better for them in the long run.

**The road less travelled**

First, I want to start with a poem which sums up the theme of this chapter really well:

## The Road Not Taken[1]
Robert Frost (1874-1963)

*Two roads diverged in a yellow wood,*
*And sorry I could not travel both*
*And be one traveller, long I stood*
*And looked down one as far as I could*
*To where it bent in the undergrowth;*
*Then took the other, as just as fair,*
*And having perhaps the better claim,*
*Because it was grassy and wanted wear;*
*Though as for that the passing there*
*Had worn them really about the same,*
*And both that morning equally lay*
*In leaves no step had trodden black.*
*Oh, I kept the first for another day!*
*Yet knowing how way leads on to way,*
*I doubted if I should ever come back.*
*I shall be telling this with a sigh*
*Somewhere ages and ages hence:*
*Two roads diverged in a wood, and I—*
*I took the one less travelled by,*
*And that has made all the difference.*

This poem has long influenced me – at least, it has justified many of the 'off-piste' decisions I've made in my own life. Although it's about someone who stands at a junction before choosing the less-travelled path, we home educators all come to points in our journeys where we have many possible paths to take, not just a choice between two. How to navigate? How to choose? What happens if we mess it up and choose wrongly?

I don't know about you, but I have these crises of confidence about

---

[1]Frost, R, 1915. *A group of poems.* The Atlantic Monthly, Washington.

once every few months! They're particularly bad over the summer, since that's when I'm trying to decide what we'll be studying for the next year. It is also particularly stressful when we hit those big rites of passage – say, moving into secondary from primary, or coming up to exam age, then Sixth Form or other routes, and finally, onwards into higher education or out into the world.

The sobering thing is that we as the parents are in charge of this! It is our responsibility: that's the very foundation of our legal ability to home-educate in the UK. Even though we will no doubt include our teens in the decision-making process, the buck will ultimately stop with us. That's scary!

So, when we get to these crossroad moments, I think it's really helpful to have a plan or a vision – a destination to aim for, if you like. If you're planning a trip to the Lake District, then you'll be looking at a map and deciding between the straight route via the motorway, or perhaps one less direct because, as is often the case, there's a huge snarl-up around Warrington. Maybe you have National Trust membership and want to stop off at one of their properties on the way, or swing by Castle Rigg and its stone circle, which is only a four-hour detour on the way to somewhere like Ambleside! If you were in the middle of studying ancient Britain, then the four-hour journey would be worth it. If you weren't, then maybe it wouldn't. You would weigh up the pros and cons.

Because we have a lot of choices in life, deciding on our destination and the ideal route to get where we want to go can be really confusing. Sifting through all the options is a parent's responsibility, and our decisions will often be based on the particular vision we have for our child's future, while perhaps also being somewhat rooted in our own pasts.

**My own journey**

It is quite a useful exercise to think about your past, especially your experience with education as you were growing up. For my part, my past heavily influenced my decisions as I worked out what I wanted for my children.

Here's how. First of all, I'm Dr Kat Patrick. Currently, I'm the

CEO of Dreaming Spires Home Learning, a tutorial company that offers live, online courses for home-educated teens worldwide, our foundational philosophy being the Charlotte Mason method (see also Appendix A). If you don't know much about Charlotte Mason, then I encourage you to check out Leah Boden's talk from the 2020 Learn Free conference.[2] Or, get a book called 'In Vital Harmony' by Karen Glass, in which she explains the philosophy and outworking of this method in a nutshell.

In addition to home-educating my children and all my tutees in the Charlotte Mason style, I also examine for Cambridge Assessment International Education for English Language IGCSEs, teach crammer courses for it and have written a revision guide, and mark their English Literature A Levels.

The 'Dr' in my name often confuses my students. It's a PhD in literary history rather than an MD, though I did actually study medicine for the first two years of my undergraduate degree. It was the prospect of taking comparative anatomy in my third year that stopped me dead in my tracks: my beloved cat had just died, and on the agenda in comparative anatomy was dissecting cats! No thank you. I just couldn't do it. So I changed to English – just like that!

Medicine to English was a big leap. If I'd grown up in the UK, I'm not sure that option would have even been open to me. The medicine pathway in England means foregoing everything but science and maths at A Level, but because I was a student in an American university, I was still enjoying a broad-based education without having burnt any bridges yet. In the US they don't so much specialise as emphasise: 35% of the whole (called a major) is focused on a specific subject like English, while the other 65% is a deliberate smorgasbord, so that a science student can write a coherent essay and an arts student can appreciate logic, accuracy and that sometimes there are such things as clear-cut right and wrong answers!

It was when I was a secondary teacher at Headington Girls' School in Oxford that it first dawned on me how much of a luxury I'd enjoyed

---

[2] https://youtu.be/dQ-xitOLcro

by having that chance to switch gears so dramatically from Medicine to English. It made me very ambivalent about the UK exam system and determined to keep a broad base of study for my own children when we got to that point.

That is the first reason that I now encourage parents to work hard to keep the delight in their teens' studies. I am scared for them. I don't want children so strait-jacketed that they get stuck in studying what they don't love and end up hating learning altogether.

To me, it's the learning – and the enjoyment of that learning – that is the point of education, rather than a piece of paper or a grade. The latter are just products with a definitive endpoint. The former is a process that never stops.

The other reason is that I just don't like exams that much. That may seem odd because I've been teaching GCSEs and A Levels for years, but the honest truth is that I do this to give home educators a short-cut so they can get it all over with, freeing them up to focus more on the good stuff.

There is more to education than parroting back a revision guide and practising past papers. Home education supposedly untethers us from these shackles. Even if your child is aiming for Oxbridge, or veterinary school, there are ways for them to delight in learning while reaching their goals – and, I would argue, sound, holistic reasons to continue with a broad-based education even while digging deeper into the things that particularly suit your child.

**Choosing a different path**

To recap the point I've been making so far: I believe that it is possible to get burned by an education that specialises too much and too early, and that it is a shame to lose out on broad-based learning that helps nurture the whole person. On top of these more universal principles, Covid-19 has thrown the exam system into a state of crisis. Now more than ever, we need that less-trodden path.

However, once we've eliminated the most popular, traditional path, which other one will we choose? This is where your 'destination' idea really comes into play, because you can't really choose which path to follow until you know where you want to end up. This may change from year to year, but keeping hold of a vision of some kind will help you work backwards to figure out the best path right now. Where is it that your child is going? What's the best way for him or her to get there?

**Pursuing natural delights: personal anecdotes**
My children started developing a clearer sense of direction at different times in their teens.

My eldest has wanted to be a writer ever since we read a book about astronauts when she was 12. All through her teen years, we kept our studies broad in the morning and left afternoons free so the children could pursue other things like music, art, crafts and playing outside. This carved out time for her to pursue her passion for writing. She published her own books on Kindle. She read voraciously. She even started her own business editing and formatting books for other people, and is now getting a big following on her 'Bookstagram' profile where she reviews young adult titles.

With her love of writing and her business acumen, she accepted a place at a US university with the idea of specialising in writing and entrepreneurship – but take 'specialise' loosely: remember that a 'major' is only 35% of the total curriculum and the other 65% is spread among other disciplines, which is why her first term included a science module in astronomy.

At the end of this term, she was contacted by the Astronomy department and asked if she would consider specialising in Astronomy alongside English. That book about astronauts – the one that inspired her to be a writer – well, we were reading it at the time because she has also always loved astronomy. She is now on course to double-specialise in English and Astronomy! That has only been possible because we didn't have to burn bridges back when she was 16.

My next child is currently 17 years old. He completely crashed out of Year 10 a few years ago. He was unmotivated, unfocused and just not producing his work. Then, the next year, something changed without any apparent reason (other than perhaps he just grew up!).

He began to apply himself in his home studies and convinced me he wouldn't blow it should he take a few modules at the local community college. He signed up for a Japanese course and because the timetable worked well, a module in electronic music composition.

What a change in this boy! It was like I'd found the electrical outlet and managed to finally plug him in. He was the youngest in his classes but getting the top grades. He found direction through them, wanting to do something like music engineering, producing or composing. I'd never seen this side of him before. Sure, he played his guitars and liked to fiddle with buttons on the sound system at church, and he also liked to play computer games and do a bit of programming and some animation, but to have a passion for something that may become a career? He even started an Instagram account where he uploads his music for the public to hear. To me, this is all a miracle.

My two younger children, a girl of 16 and a boy of 14, are still exploring their options. It looks like they may lean toward the sciences, so I have let my daughter sign up for two science courses every year for the past couple of years. Before Covid, these would be one with our local home education co-operative group and the other online with Dreaming Spires. Now, one is with Dreaming Spires and the other is something we do together, like health and nutrition. My youngest added more science exploration by doing monthly activity boxes (KiwiCo) and spending his TV time with VSauce, Slo-Mo Guys and Smarter Every Day.

For them, I feel that we're still in a 'watch this space' season. Those passions may change, but the passion itself is what excites me – it belies curiosity and a desire to learn.

The reason this excites me is that as parents, we will never be able to teach our children everything they need to know before they leave home. Even if every waking moment was spent teaching, we'd still only scratch the surface. I mean, think about how much you're learning alongside your children. You clearly didn't learn everything you needed to know before 18! In the same way, there's no end date for their learning, and learning via their natural delights is the way to keep them eager to learn for the rest of their lives.

**General principles for delight-led learning**

So, how do we do this? The short answer is: however suits your own children! Saying that, I think there are some general principles that you might find helpful as you navigate your options.

The first one is to stay broad in their studies. What that looks like in practice is up to you; for me, it means using the Charlotte Mason method (see also Appendix A), adapted for secondary schooling. It's perhaps a little less broad than for under-14s, but it's still rich with great books, ideas and discussion.

The second principle is to allow for some 'unschooling', or "masterly inactivity" as Charlotte Mason talks about (1904, p.25): those afternoons for exploration after a morning of more formal or structured learning. These could involve listening to music or reading for fun, doing activities or experiments. I would recommend that this one portion of the day be kept free of electronics or screens, but that is a whole different discussion!

Thirdly, and crucially – this is a huge oversight in so many teens' education, both schooled and home-educated – keep at least some part of their education relational: with YOU! Be involved. Talk things over. Read a book aloud together at night instead of letting everyone go to their rooms and do their own thing. My heart aches for children who are pointed toward a huge pile of books and told to work their way through them. The lack of buy-in from their parents must be soul-destroying, or at least, put nagging doubts in their heads that learning is a chore which children must do, but which adults would never bother with.

If I were to incorporate this idea of delight-directed learning into our metaphor about choosing which path to take, it would look something like this: choose the path full of delightful sights, smells, sounds and textures (i.e. broad-based studies); give your children the chance to meander off the beaten track and explore some things on their own (i.e. the empty hours for a teen to fill with their own projects); always be present as their guide, who is on the journey with them: be the one to whom the child can return to show that froglet, that caterpillar, that fresh-picked wild apple that you can each take bites of, that dewdrop captured on a leaf.

That's why I think it's so important to make sure our destination is not primarily GCSEs, A Levels, Scottish Highers, or university degrees, but the journey of learning itself. Learning to learn. Nurturing their curiosity is the ideal destination, because it outlives the short years that we have with our children and sets them up for what is to come.

You can travel toward this destination in hundreds of different ways. Remember that trip to the Lake District? We talked about the motorway or the A-roads, but why stop there? What about a train or a bike or a hot air balloon – what about a gigantic drone that can carry you? You're limited only by your imagination, and it's the journey that feeds this curiosity.[3]

Don't get me wrong: I'm not saying that taking the motorway is bad. Assuming that by the motorway we all understand that I'm talking about the usual exam system, I would never advise anyone not to do exams at all. I do feel very strongly, however, that exams should not be the only focus. They can be so prescriptive and there are so many other ways to enjoy better learning opportunities.

## Popular alternative pathways

I am assuming, of course, that most of you reading this are in agreement, at least in principle; otherwise, I doubt you would have headed toward the 'part of the woods' with the interesting pathways in the first place. You probably know intuitively that there is something more than the traditional education system, and perhaps are reading

---

[3] This reminds me of Ken Robinson's TED talk about changing paradigms in education. Studies show that younger children have more imaginative solutions for things than older children who have been 'educated' into conformity. It's worth a watch: https://www.ted.com/talks/sir_ken_robinson_changing_education_paradigms

this book to find out what options there are. I can't cover all of them, because there are as many choices in pathways as you can imagine! But for the sake of argument, let's look a few of the more popular ones.

The first pathway is where students take *some* exams, while putting effort into other enjoyable and stimulating projects along the way. The exam shortlist may include subjects we consider essential, like English Language and Maths, but others could also be undertaken.

Some, however, require wise consideration. Certain history syllabuses, for example, have become so bloated that they need three years of study just to cover all the topics. Is that really a good use of one's learning? Even someone who loves history might be better served by foregoing an exam and, instead, studying the subject for its own sake. With that comes the freedom to make connections oneself between eras, or to be inspired by a particular leader or revolutionary, or even by simpler, gentler characters who didn't make the exam syllabus because their impact wasn't considered important by the exam board.

In other words, just because a student likes a subject, it may not be the wisest decision to take an exam in it.

Another consideration when choosing which exams to take and which subjects to study just for enjoyment, is whether or not it is a sensible exam, a complicated exam, one that requires too many hoops to be jumped through, or one which has poor outcomes. Once such example is ICT which, for some years, has proven disastrous for home educators when exam centres have provided the wrong equipment, not had accessible printers, or ordered the wrong exam papers. It is important to weigh up the benefits and costs of each exam, and I don't just mean the monetary cost.

As a second possible pathway, there are some activities and programmes that are counted as qualification equivalents, like the Art Award or music grades. I always found the art awards very stimulating. When my daughter did hers, she composed a piece of violin music called 'Murmurations' and her project was a big basket-woven sphere with origami birds all over it. We actually included this item in our shipment of furniture when we moved overseas a few years ago, it was that precious.

New qualifications are appearing all the time, but also disappearing all the time, too, so these need to be undertaken with some caution. For example, there used to be a wonderful nutrition course designed by Jamie Oliver and run as a BTEC by Pearson, but alas, it has been discontinued. Some of the videos are still found on YouTube, but the course booklet (which some home educators would print out and undertake at home for the fun of it) is no longer accessible.

Other qualifications, like national foreign language exams that, say, France and Spain offer, may not be accepted for UCAS points, but they are internationally recognised for language proficiency and, arguably, carry more weight in the working world.

As a third pathway, more and more home educators are turning to the broad-based American system and US SATs as an alternative route to UK university (there is a whole Facebook group called 'HE Success without UK exams' in which parents who have done this are on hand to give advice about the process).

The US system bypasses GCSEs altogether (though that doesn't mean you can't choose to do some anyway – remember, this is YOUR path). Basically, you spend about four years studying a broad-based curriculum and keep a portfolio of grades (I have a couple of videos on YouTube about how to do this[4]). At some point toward the end of the four years, you register for the US SAT general exam. It's a multiple-choice exam focusing on literacy and numeracy, taken on a single Saturday, costing around £100 or less. It helps to do some specific revision for it, but thankfully there are revision books and even courses, like those available online at Khan Academy, that will coach the child to the answers.

It often isn't an indication of their knowledge so much as their mastery of the game. I don't have a problem with this. The real learning happens in the preceding four years when subjects can be studied holistically, realistically, relationally and in context.

---

[4] https://youtube.com/playlist?list=PLPaEPwdHni4kQKI83oBRV5W22hLY-bNHcx

I have not commented in this section on vocational options, which provide a whole host of other possibilities (I am not well versed in these, but there is no doubt a Facebook group about them!). Instead, and finally, I want to touch on an alternative route to university as a mature student. This route begins as young as 21, allowing countless possibilities a young adult could explore and enjoy prior to that: a job, volunteering, missionary work, entrepreneurship. All these experiences are valid elements of a university application, perhaps even obviating the need for any exams at all. That will depend, of course, on the subject one wants to study, but you can imagine a young person diving into the deep end of drama through hands-on experiences at theatres, then applying for a Drama course as a mature student once they are over 21.

It would be remiss of me if I didn't briefly flag up the many outsourced courses and tutorials which can be found, both as local in-person groups and online, whether taught live or via videos. As people plan their pathways, there are usually some subjects which a student loves but a parent has less confidence in teaching it. In these instances, it would probably make sense to find someone to take over for you. Not all courses are the same, though: some companies offer a course and then find somebody to teach the pre-made curriculum on their behalf. Some provide only pre-recorded videos, some are delivered live by the person who actually wrote the webinars, and everything in between.

My own experience has been that only the live-taught ones will keep my children's interest week by week, all year long. Once again, you have to pick the pathway that suits your children, your purse and your schedule the best.

**Nurturing a love of learning**

As this chapter draws to its end, I want to recap: your teens are at a stage of exploration and discovery, and it is your responsibility to help them through it. I believe the destination during secondary home education should be learning to learn, so that, when they do find their passion in life, they will have the curiosity, tools, skills and mindset to help them nurture it.

There are many, many pathways to achieve this goal. It is my belief that the well-worn path of focusing solely on UK exams is less satisfying and stimulating than one which makes at least some room for beautiful scenery and exploration.

As I established earlier, these are ideas that not only come from my own personal and professional experiences (and even my fears) as a home-educating mum, but they also come from my observations of home educators over the years who, frankly, freak out about secondary school and, so many times, give up their lovely family journey of learning together to put their teen into school, or into a school-at-home situation.

There are alternatives to this that are just as good, if not better. Don't be afraid to choose the road less travelled; I believe it will make all the difference.

CHAPTER THREE

# SOCIALLY SPEAKING: UNDERSTANDING THE HOME-EDUCATED CHILD AS A SOCIAL BEING

*Juliet English*

"I'm stupid!"

I glanced into the rear-view mirror at my daughter's downcast face as we drove out of the school gates. Her outburst was upsetting – a parent would not want their 7-year-old to even think such a thing, let alone express it. I knew that I needed to act, and soon, or these thoughts would erode her confidence and become part of her identity.

The year was 1997, and my daughter was attending a school we were generally happy with. It was not too big, had a nurturing culture and a friendly, enlightened atmosphere. My daughter had friends and seemed to be performing satisfactorily. Sometimes, on a Monday, she would announce that her tummy hurt; we eventually figured out that she had PE on a Monday and the teacher responsible had a somewhat 'shouty' way of communicating with the children which made my daughter anxious. After finding out from other parents that she was not the only one affected in this way, we wrote to the headteacher to express our concerns about our daughter potentially being put off PE for the rest of her childhood due to this. However, nothing seemed to change, so we were left trying to figure out how to best support our daughter.

This statement from her, however, was new, and to a parent concerned with her child's wellbeing, it was not something to be dismissed or ignored. Cue further conversations with the school, still with no satisfactory results. We wanted our daughter to have a happy and 'successful' experience, to achieve her potential, but didn't feel like we had any control over what happened at school. Happily, discovering that home education was an option and meeting other home educators resulted in a decision we have never regretted!

Casting my mind back to that time, I don't remember ever being concerned about whether our children's social needs would be met, and it was certainly never a factor in our decision to home-educate.

However, we were to hear the same question time and time again, with disappointing frequency, from friends, family and totally random strangers: "But what about socialisation?" We heard it so many times that we used to joke that we should keep a pre-recorded response handy to play back on cue!

**What is socialisation and should I be concerned about it?**

Whilst definitions can vary, there is general consensus among the different dictionaries I have consulted that socialisation refers to the process, beginning during childhood, by which individuals acquire the values, habits and attitudes of a culture or society. It is most easily likened to the process you might use to train a young puppy to cope with different situations and people – exposing them to a variety of experiences in a safe manner.

If you're talking about this definition of socialisation, then you'll find that most caring parents do this naturally, helping their children find appropriate ways to behave and respond as they go about their normal activities together. For a child attending school, a teacher might assume a similar role.

However, what people usually mean when they use the term socialisation is 'socialising' or social interaction with others. There is often an assumption that, just because children are not in a group of others the same age for several hours a day, they are somehow being deprived of the opportunity to be social. Some will even imply that your child is likely to grow up 'weird', 'socially awkward' or shy, unable to hold a conversation, or work with a group.

**Socialisation in schools**

Whilst I would not want to encourage casting school in a negative light – your child may need to attend one again at some stage – I think it is important to question what social interaction (or 'socialisation' if we must use the word) looks like for many children within a school setting, and its impact on the individual child. Here are some points to consider:

1. No teacher, no matter how well meaning, comes to the role devoid of values, culture, worldview, or even emotional baggage. These will leak through in their communications with children, and in the values they seek to instil in their classes – whether they are positive or negative.

2. The 2020 Good Childhood Report from the Children's Society found that children in the UK have the lowest levels of life satisfaction in Europe, with a particularly British fear of failure partly to blame (p.44), and that the UK has some of the highest levels of schoolwork pressure on 15-year-olds (p.44). It also states that 23% of UK girls "had low wellbeing [scores] on at least three out of four measures (life satisfaction, happiness, sadness and sense of purpose) compared to 14% of boys" (p.48). As a result of the Covid-19 lockdown, many parents chose to continue educating their children at home, due to improved mental health, academic performance and family relationships.

3. Bullying has become prevalent in school culture and is a daily challenge for many children in school. Besides the obvious physical bullying, which can reach seriously harmful levels, children might experience verbal, emotional and sexual abuse, which could be in person, or via social media and messaging. Although a lot of bullying may happen between peers, it is not unusual for staff members to be perpetrators as well.

4. The teenage years are really a time in a young person's life when they should be learning to take on more responsibility, kept busy and active, and encouraged in their interests as they begin considering their future as adults. However, the school system arguably keeps them as children during this crucial time and treats them as if they are unable to think for themselves. Often, expectations are low, and mediocrity is celebrated. Silly little reward systems are just another box-ticking exercise, and a manipulative tool that children see right through.

For many people (myself included), school might have been a really positive experience, where they thrived academically, emotionally and socially. It is often these sorts of experiences which have them questioning whether a home-educated child is being deprived of something they personally enjoyed.

However, not all schools or school experiences will necessarily be alike, and in the UK, long school days, a narrow curriculum that is disconnected from the real world, and increased pressure to perform (with little emphasis on mastery and enjoyment), leave little time to cultivate meaningful friendships. Whilst it is true that a child will be placed in a group of children around the same age as themselves, it is a forced association which doesn't reflect the society they are likely to enter as adults – a society in which they will come across people of all ages and backgrounds. There will invariably be some children for whom the 'one-size-fits-all' environment can be stressful, sometimes even harmful, and therefore not conducive to learning and thriving.

## 'Vertical' socialisation

On leaving school and possibly university, most young people will need to be able to work with others both older and younger than themselves. The home-educating family provides great preparation for this and can ensure that the child is exposed to 'real life' and society in a more natural way. Even a family of introverts will generally be out and about in their community, shopping, visiting doctors/dentists, going to the park, etc. As the child observes the parent interacting with others, they become comfortable in the company of adults, as well as children of all ages. In home education circles, we refer to 'vertical socialisation' as opposed to 'horizontal socialisation' – the former means the ability to relate to and converse with people both older and younger than oneself. Parents can facilitate a safe environment for the child to learn appropriate behaviour and conversational skills.

In our large family of seven children, the older children have always played happily with their younger siblings, and sometimes helped take care of them. The younger siblings, in turn, are used to being around big brother or sister and their friends. They are expected to be patient and treat each other kindly. It doesn't always work, but that's the idea. One of my younger daughters always had a bit of a 'Pied Piper' effect, in that little children followed her around and loved to sit with her and watch her draw.

## Teenagers and peer groups

In respect of teenagers, some might argue that the peer group is important. But there is also potential for it to be a very harmful environment during those vulnerable, self-conscious years, stuck between childhood and adulthood, with limited input from caring adults. Many an adult pays the price for foolish behaviour as a teenager.

I have observed that my children have not always found it easy to get along with children their own age who attend school. Often, schooled children seem to be caught up in the world of playground politics, bullying behaviour, the desire to show off, and crude talk. It seems, in modern schools, that young people grow up disconnected from the adult world, and that behaviour is tolerated that would be regarded as unacceptable in the workplace. One of my daughters started going to a running club, and soon found that she had more in common with the adults than children her own age and complained that "All they want to talk about is sex and boys", when she preferred talking about politics and current events. She found her college classmates to be childish, crude and disrespectful, but was completely comfortable chatting to her tutors.

Our young people are often involved in fairly grown-up conversations about world affairs, relationships and life challenges. They are able to observe more of adult life in action as they are with their parents for significant periods of time and can talk with their parents about their interests and ideas. This has had a really positive outcome, as I've observed my children learning to articulate their thoughts and converse with curiosity and intelligence. It's a real pleasure to watch my children at college interviews – confident, articulate and enthused about their subject – with the interviewer clearly impressed and eager to sign them up! I gather it's a surprising change after interviewing one grunting teen after another, some of whom seem to have no idea why they're there!

## Preparing for the 'real' world

Home-educated young people pick up on how their parents behave and interact. If a parent demonstrates leadership, entrepreneurship, confidence, charitable work, generosity and a good work ethic, it is very likely the child will emulate the same traits, just as they might any negative traits. For me, as a home educator, I've been learning right alongside my children, and become excited by things I've learnt – which then excites them too! Parents have a significant role to play in how we influence the course of our children's lives. The home provides a safe environment for them to make mistakes, and learn, and grow.

Home education creates independent thinkers, encourages children to take initiative, to manage themselves and to prize meaningful engagement. One of my daughters was appointed as a college ambassador within six months of enrolment and has been commended by her college for her willingness to assist other students and take the initiative. Yet another serves as a student representative at university and assisted at the University Covid-19 testing centres (whilst working part-time and building up her own business).

When my children receive recognition from the outside world, naturally I am proud of them, but I also tell them that I am quite unsurprised, as I know that they are just being who they are. Giving them a solid foundation in common sense, guiding them towards independent thinking and encouraging their individual gifts and talents enables them to stand out, without even trying. This seems to be true of almost every home-educated family I've ever come across.

**Finding a community**

It's hard enough choosing to go against the norm, but without support, and with others questioning your competence and your ability to make good decisions for your children, taking that huge step to home education can seem even more daunting. Finding a supportive and encouraging community is hugely important for parents and children and can make all the difference to how you experience home education.

Parents will find it helpful to talk to others who have more experience, and to seek advice from them. It helps to affirm them in their decision to home-educate and prevent feelings of loneliness and isolation. Children have opportunities to connect with others, of all ages, who are home-educated like themselves, participate in group activities and experience social interaction in a free and natural way, with parents on hand to facilitate and guide if needed.

Home education support groups arise out of different needs. They can cater for a specific academic or extra-curricular need (for example, STEM groups [Science, Technology, Engineering and Mathematics], art, drama or sport). Many groups meet so that children have the opportunity to participate in group activities, such as crafts, and thus also fulfil a social need.

Groups that meet regularly and which have good, consistent leadership may find that, for many of their members, they become a strong support community. As friendships between members develop and are strengthened, it may become possible to provide much more than just a 'mutual interest' group. It can become a place where children feel accepted and have a sense of belonging, where they have friends to hang out with, and where parents are encouraged and empowered.

Home education groups can now be found all over the UK, and social media has made finding local groups a simple matter of typing in "home education *your area*". If you are fortunate, you will find that there are already active, thriving support groups not far from where you live and that's a good place to start.

However, sometimes it can be a challenge finding a group that is the right 'fit' for you and your children and there is nothing to stop you from starting your own group. With home education growing as steadily as it is, there is always a need for more support groups. A group may fulfil the needs of one child, but not of another; there is no need to feel like the groups are 'competing' with each other – indeed, in many areas of the UK, home education groups may co-exist in a region quite happily, with overlap of members, allowing for the different needs of individuals. Appendix B lays out a wealth of practical advice on starting and running successful home education support groups.

## Equipped for life

The vehicle of home education provides a wonderful opportunity for caring parents to instil solid foundations in their children's lives as they support them not only in their learning, but in their development as social beings. A child who enjoys the consistent rhythms of home, unconditional acceptance, appropriate boundaries and balance, and authentic support and encouragement through all stages of their growth and development, while being exposed simultaneously to the society they are part of, is likely to be well equipped to deal with all its benefits and challenges as an adult.

CHAPTER FOUR

# BUT WHERE WILL THE WHITEBOARD GO?! MOVING FROM SCHOOL EDUCATION TO HOME EDUCATION

*Siân Lowe*

"So, I'm thinking of home-schooling ..."
Sitting in a friend's living room, drinking coffee with a couple of other school-mum friends after a typical morning school run, the words coming out of my mouth sounded so alien. And yet, what a relief to have finally said it. Out loud. This was my safe place, with people I loved and trusted, to test the waters before braving the many different responses of others to this strange phenomenon commonly known as 'home schooling'. If you have already taken your child out of school, you will undoubtedly be familiar with other people's thoughts on your decision to educate your child in a different way. If you have yet to take the leap, I hope this chapter gives you some idea of what to expect.

Taking your child out of the school system is considered by many a very 'brave' thing to do. And with good reason. For most of us, the transition from school to home school (or 'home education', which is the term preferred by most home educators in the UK) will require courage, a thick skin, and a willingness to fail in order to succeed, whatever you consider 'success' to mean. And at times the pressure of being responsible for your child's education will more than likely weigh heavily – very heavily – as you swim against the tide of formal education. So, why would anyone put themselves through it?

Why indeed. We all have a 'why' – for some that 'why' may stand proudly, deeply rooted, able to withstand any storm; for others it may just be a seed that has recently been sown. In her book, 'The Call of the Wild and Free' (2019, p.18), Ainsley Arment talks about the importance of knowing your 'why':

> *Everyone needs a 'why' to make it through the difficult times, the seemingly unfruitful times, the times when you question your decision ... Your 'why' is your reason. Your 'why' is the conviction that inspires you and fuels the passion within you ... Your 'why' gives you the ability to inspire your children and guide them on this journey.*

We didn't want a 'why'. We certainly weren't looking for a 'why'. And yet, my husband Matt and I nevertheless found ourselves contemplating removing our children from an education system that had educated us, served us well and to which I had devoted years of my working life. Our 'why' felt pretty much imposed on us at first – an unwelcome visitor in our lives. But as we learned to embrace it, it began to grow into something increasingly beautiful. And so in this chapter I simply intend to share the story of our transition from school education to home education, in the hope that it will encourage and inform you – whatever stage of the journey you may be on.

**A niggling suspicion**

So, back to the beginning. I had been a secondary schoolteacher and senior leader for many years before we adopted our three amazing daughters who, for their sakes, we will refer to as Rosabella, Ivy and Princess Sophia (their choice of names, not mine!). Home education was not on our radar at all as we moved to a bigger house in the heart of the school community in preparation for family life. At first, we enjoyed being immersed in the school world and were reassured by the friendly and kind nature of the teachers. It didn't take long, however, for the emotional needs of our girls to become evident. As a 'fixer', I threw myself into working with the school to raise awareness of the needs of adopted children and to encourage a more informed response.

Training for all staff was provided, significant time was given to parents and teachers for regular in-depth discussions, transition from one teacher to the next was handled with greater sensitivity, an adoptive parents' group was formed and guidelines were put in place. A great, big, massive 'tick' for all concerned! I am grateful to this day for how the school responded to this persistent but always polite parent – well, that's how I viewed myself, at least!

So, surely now we could relax? For a little while, perhaps – had it not been for an ever-increasing niggle, a growing suspicion that maybe our girls did not fit into the education system or meet its expectations. It was a niggle I tried hard to suppress – our girls were OK, weren't they? Friendships were a bit hit-and-miss, academic progress wasn't quite in line with their year groups, but overall, it wasn't so bad. We had a good relationship with the school, and what about my lovely mum friends and the girls' play dates? "It'll be OK, it'll be OK ... this is school life ... we'll get them through ..."

**A pressing need**

And then came dyslexia. Glorious, wonderful dyslexia. It was clear by the end of Year 2 that our eldest, Rosabella, was not 'catching up'. Spelling tests ruled our evenings, reading logs became the bane of our lives and we watched over the next two years as our wonderful, sparky daughter lost faith in herself. Watching her pretend to read out a poem with the rest of her class in front of parents is still, for me, a heart-breaking memory. And even then, I was sure that this too could be fixed. But after much research, I was dismayed to discover how little effective support was offered to dyslexics in primary schools. Rosabella was put on a waiting list for an assessment that never came. Understandably, other children with greater needs were given priority, but it meant that we were left stranded. Matt and I invested in an online reading programme, which we completed at home after school each day, and met regularly with caring but overstretched teachers to discuss how best to support her progress and build her confidence. Our combined efforts were, to be blunt, fruitless. The system just did not have the funding or resources to help us fix this problem.

Unsurprisingly, as Rosabella started Year 4, the home-educating niggle just grew and grew. Suddenly I was aware of the existence of home educators, real people out there living outside of the school system. But home education still seemed a terrifying prospect. We were blessed to be put in touch with a relatively new home-educating family who reassured us that making the decision was the hardest bit. They certainly weren't looking back. So, after much prayer and following another 'I'm rubbish' meltdown, I took a deep breath and suggested to Rosabella that we could home-educate instead. What a relief when she came back with an emphatic 'No!'. Well, God, I tried; what can I say? But deep inside, I still knew that home education was where we were heading ...

Poetry week was the straw that broke the camel's back. It wasn't enough to simply enjoy a poem: it had to be memorised and recited in class, with the best of the performers chosen to recite the poem in assembly to great applause from all the unchosen. In the interest of inclusivity but without any hope of great applause, Rosabella had been tasked with memorising just three lines. Driving back from a lovely family day out, all three girls were going over their lines. We were on a hiding to nothing. The pressure of those three lines was just too much. Rosabella broke down and I felt a quiet divine prompt to gently say, "There's always home schooling." "Yes, that's what I want", came the reply, and the sobbing stopped. Matt and I exchanged a look that was half terror, half quiet acceptance, and that was that. We gave Rosabella a few months' grace to change her mind, but just like another strong-minded female you may have heard of, this girl was not for turning!

We used those few months to begin a conversation with the headteacher about leaving school. When it became clear that Rosabella would indeed be leaving at the end of the academic year, discussions turned to how she could leave well. Being this transparent with school may not be the right thing for everyone who wants to remove their child, but given the regular communication that had taken place since day one of reception, we knew this was the right way forward. To honour the relationship we had with school was important to us. And school did us proud. Rosabella left with all the best wishes one could hope for. I cried; she didn't.

**Navigating questions and comments**

The summer came and went and, in all honesty, I didn't give an awful lot of thought as to what I would be doing with Rosabella come the start of the autumn term. She had left school, but her sisters were going back; Matt and I were still dealing with our own response to that as well as fielding all the questions and comments that came our way from friends and family, most of which we didn't have answers to! And breathe ... Maybe here is a good place to pause and say a word or two about those questions and comments.

If you choose to home-educate, get used to it: questions and comments from other people will be a part of your life – even from complete strangers! In our experience, most of the time, comments come from genuine curiosity and some have been wonderfully encouraging and affirming. It would be a fun exercise to gather from UK home educators a Top Ten list of the most frequent comments they have received! The most common we hear is, "I could never do it", a loaded comment driven either by fear, or by admiration, or a mixture of both, depending on how satisfied that person is with the mainstream education system. "You're so brave" is another, to which my response in the early days was, "Yes, I am!" followed by a slightly hysterical giggle. "I couldn't spend all day with my children" is another favourite, and one that I'm still never sure how to respond to, so I don't. "You're a teacher so you can do it, but I wouldn't know where to start" is the one that makes me laugh out loud, because it should make perfect sense. "No, no, I don't know what to do!!" is what I wanted to scream in the early days, knowing even then that being a home educator would be a very different thing to being a secondary state-school teacher. Reluctant teenage learners taller than me I can cope with, but home education?!

What about friends; what will you do with them? How will you follow the school curriculum? What about socialisation? What if they fall behind? What about GCSEs? What about Art? How will you teach science? Where will the whiteboard go?! The list goes on and on. But at the end of the day, whether these questions are asked from concern, curiosity, or just undisguised criticism, as a new or imminent home educator, they can be unsettling and unnerving. But remember this: when you step outside of the norm, it can be unsettling not just for you, but for those around you as well. I'm not great with change; I'm better than I used to be, but generally I like predictability and familiarity and I'd prefer it if everyone else would just stay the same as well, thank you very much. I don't know about you, but if a friend moves away, I struggle. I want to be happy for them, but the truth is, I liked them living where they lived, near me. If they're moving, should we be moving? Are we missing out or are we OK where we are? Maybe this inner questioning just highlights my own insecurities, but I do wonder if, when someone else makes a change or steps out into something different, it provides us with an opportunity to review where we're at in life and what God may be saying to us. This is how I choose to view the comments I receive about home education.

Within your school community, some parents will be perfectly happy with the provision for their children and so will either think you have lost the plot, or simply be very happy for you. For others, it will cause them to consider in greater depth their child's school experience and what they want for them; having paused to review it all, they will either happily continue as is or watch you closely to see how you get on. And for others, there may just be plain regret that this is something they are not able to do right now. Whatever the response, my advice is to try to respond with an awareness of what may be going on for that person. It's very much a relational thing.

Back then, with those who I knew had our best interests at heart and who mean a lot to us, it was good to take the time to talk it all through, remembering that ultimately it was our decision. With others whose motive for questioning I was less sure about, a quick, "Oh, it's just something we want to try to help Rosabella with her confidence – we'll see how it goes" was sufficient, followed by a change of subject if needed. I tried hard to be me, to not hide my nervousness, to be real, to say, "I don't know" when I didn't. "If you see us banging on the school doors come October, let us in!" was my parting plea as we finished the summer term. Most people respond well to vulnerability, I find, and boy, did I feel vulnerable.

**De-schooling**

So, we had taken the leap. What next? In a word – 'de-schooling'. Not a term I had heard of before home education entered our lives! But I quickly heard all about it from home-educating friends. De-schooling is the time you give your child to adapt to not being at school. Some children need time not only to adapt, but to recover from their school experience. The general guidance is to give your child one month for each year they attended school to relax into this new way of living, before attempting to work out a home-education schedule or rhythm.

Not only was this great advice, but it was also very convenient, as I had no idea what to do or how to start Rosabella's home education. De-schooling, I found, is just as much about the parent as it is about the child, especially for a former schoolteacher. The first two weeks were strange, but manageable. I still had to do the school run with Ivy and Princess Sophia, and initially Rosabella would accompany us. Too weird. I felt the weirdness for both Rosabella and myself as she waved to her former classmates. We didn't do much, aside from reading together on the sofa (me reading of course), an hour once a week at the Dyslexia Centre and working through a maths book

(I know, I know, but it made me feel better that there was some 'proper' learning going on). And before you knew it, it was school run time and a chance for us both to feel weird again as Rosabella hunted down any friends who may have stayed behind to play in the playground. But it was all OK. Really, it was. I found that we talked a lot, and about important stuff too – educational stuff, some may even say! I enjoyed our time together and so I pushed the weirdness away.

The floodgates opened at the end of those two weeks. I came home from an evening out to Matt very casually informing me that Rosabella couldn't sleep as she had changed her mind about home education. Changed her mind?! What do you mean, changed her mind? What else did she say? Did she say why? What exactly were her words? What did you say? What do we do now?! Fortunately, my husband is very used to my loud external processing. I found the grown-up in me, went to find my daughter and held her calmly while she sobbed about missing her friends, and please could I phone the headteacher and get her place back. I prayed for her, soothed her to sleep and then didn't sleep myself – for another two weeks. I had crumpled. I felt my daughter's loss and I found it hard to bear. She had lost enough in life as it was. I don't know how you cope in times of doubt and trouble, but I prayed my heart out. Had we got it wrong, Lord? Had we not heard correctly? What were we to do now?

We talked it all through with Rosabella and landed on a deal that we would give it until Christmas and then review, because really, we couldn't know if home education was the right thing or not after just two weeks. That worked, and Rosabella found her form again, but it had rocked me for sure. Looking back, I can see that it was only natural that there would be a honeymoon period, but that friends would then be missed and that my daughter would have doubts and down days as she settled into being with … well, me. One morning, after we had both ended up weeping on the sofa together, I declared that times like this require a visit to my happy place. Intrigued, Rosabella jumped into the car with me, and we drove to a lovely lido and café in an affluent part of town, with cakes that cost more than they should and where children are rarely seen. The sun was shining and, despite being told that they had run out of egg custard tarts, Rosabella's favourite, one was miraculously found. As we settled down to cake, lemonade and reading our book, 'Don't worry, be happy' started to play out of the speakers. It was one of those moments when you feel God's blessing and you just know that it's all going to be alright.

From then on, Rosabella and I settled into a relaxed rhythm of being at home. She no longer did the school runs with us (we had figured out that meeting schoolfriends individually was better than in a group to avoid all the school talk) and took up chess! She started at forest school one day a week with the children of other home-educating families we had met, and joined a home-education trampolining group; we also had a weekly meet-up at the library with a home-educating mum and her son to whom we had been introduced and who sparked her interest in chess. In time, audiobooks, listening to music and touch-typing also joined the list of activities, along with a newly formed drama group – we were off! Aside from working through our maths book, no formal learning or teaching took place. And it felt good.

## Challenges and encouragements

Now, this is not to say that it was all plain sailing. Wobbles came and went (they still do) and as a stay-at-home mum, it was hard at times to accept the loss of the weekly rhythm I had developed during school hours. I didn't like my lack of availability for friends, family, or anything else for that matter. I missed my coffee times, those times when as friends you put each other back together, laugh at life or just find comfort in knowing that it's not just you. Housework became a random activity; online grocery shopping became the norm and finances had to be reprioritised to fund the various groups. Rosabella was giving it her best and working hard at adapting to living in the heart of a school community whilst no longer being a part of it – not easy with her sisters waving goodbye each morning. But we were definitely getting there.

Two months into all of this, my father came to visit. Now Dad is a retired headteacher and, whilst he hadn't shared any massive concern or shock over our decision to take Rosabella out of school, I suspected that he was keeping his worries to himself. All three of us spent the afternoon together and then I left the two of them to it to pick up Ivy and Princess Sophia from school. Over a cup of tea later on, while the girls were watching TV, conversation turned to home education. Dad began ominously, saying that he hadn't understood what we were doing taking Rosabella out of school ... deep breath, here it comes ... but that he completely 'got it' now. I stared at him. "She's a different girl. Her eyes are so bright now." I could have wept (not sure why I didn't, I usually weep given half a chance) – those words were the best encouragement to keep going that I could have hoped for. He could see what I had suspected was there but what I hadn't dared to declare. A new energy, increased confidence, a spark in Rosabella that had returned.

**No regrets**

That first year was passing quickly and, along with the relief that life was progressing as well as we could have hoped, there was a new feeling brewing inside. 'This is good. This feels right. This is how I want us to live, all of us.' Having one foot in and one foot out of school wasn't really how Matt and I wanted to do life, and it wasn't as though Ivy and Princess Sophia were flying high at school. They both processed the offer of home education in their own unique way, and both agreed to give it a go. This time, we took them out just after May half-term, to avoid all the transition to new groups that takes place in that final term. We celebrated by going on holiday in term-time – it just had to be done!

So, there we were, a fully signed-up home-educating family.

That was three years ago. Since then, there have been the inevitable ups and downs, various lockdowns and a move away from our community and friends. I have wobbled many times and occasionally fantasised about the girls getting on a bus and going back to school, leaving the responsibility of their education to someone else! But I have also delighted in our time together and in watching them grow as individuals. I am so utterly grateful for the privilege of being able to home-educate. We have found the things that work for us and have also found that these change along the way. And we have also realised that what works for us is unique to us; I can still at times fall into that awful trap of anxiously comparing what we do to what other families do. But I'm much stronger in who we are as a family than I was at the beginning of this journey, when I was just a bag of nerves and questions!

Do Matt and I regret making the transition from school education to home education? No. Not one bit. Not for all the wobbles. What is more, our 'why' has grown and developed from those early dyslexia-driven days. This is time we will never have again. Time for us as a family, time for our girls to work out at their own pace their strengths and talents – who God created them to be. Time to talk, to read, to have shared experiences. Time to understand what learning really is. Time to enjoy learning.

And as for the whiteboard? We never have figured out where it should go ...

## CHAPTER FIVE

# ADDITIONAL NEEDS: MAKING ROOM FOR DISABILITIES, DISORDERS, DIFFICULTIES AND DIFFERENCES

*Anne Laure Jackson*

How do we thrive in home education when someone in the household has a disability, a disorder, a dysfunction, or another kind of difference? The mum – the dad – a child – the children – struggling with needs and not being so-called 'normal'? It brings up so many questions, doesn't it!

Fears and concerns can easily flood in. Even under 'normal' circumstances we ask ourselves anxious questions like, 'Can I home-educate?' 'Can I make it work?' 'Will I be enough?' 'Can I really do it?'

Then we need to add in another layer of self-doubt if someone has additional needs ...

- 'What I fail them?'
- 'What if I don't meet their needs?'
- 'What about the specialist help?'
- 'Can I trust myself that they will they turn out alright?'
- 'What does that diagnosis mean for us?'
- 'What does our home education look like now?'
- 'I just want to be the same as everyone else!'

And the list goes on.

Before I go any further, can I just say: YES! You will be enough, you can do it, and yes, your children will thrive!

What is more, even though it covers some tough issues, I hope that this chapter will support you to make the most of your home educating. I write it as a home-educating mum of 20 years and hope to take you a little through my personal journey first, then my professional journey as an occupational therapist with families I love and serve whose children are on various spectrums of disability, disorder and difference; then I'll offer my tuppence of advice at the end.

Much of what you'll read is coming from my own personal journey of faith and my own transformation while home educating through my specific family circumstances, which I hope will be an encouragement to you if your family looks different to the norm. If the Christian faith is not your foundation, however, I hope that the offerings in this chapter will still be helpful and thought-provoking for you.

## My story: home educating with spousal disability

I knew my husband was 'different' before we got married, but I had no idea how this was going to impact our lives together at the time. Every single day we face new challenges and together we learn how to handle them and grow in many different ways as we journey in parenting and marriage with the diagnosis of a visual impairment and multiple sclerosis (MS). MS is an incurable and degenerative disability, and unless there is supernatural or breakthrough medical intervention, the condition will cause a deterioration in my husband's function for the rest of his life – and our lives together. He started losing obvious function years ago when our eldest child was then 5 years old, and we never know now what each day will bring. Our children have also seen and lived with the deterioration.

For us, the decline in what my husband has been able to do and be has been slow but steady. First, his eyes went blind (for a time). Next, his arms and legs stopped functioning so that he couldn't write or walk (again, for a time). Then there were the pins and needles and the parts of his body going numb; then the physical tiredness and brain fog; then it was the forgetfulness and the repetition of questions, and so it goes on. It wasn't and isn't easy for him, or us.

It's not fun for the children; neither is it fun being the dad who can't catch a ball with his sons, kick a football, drive his boys anywhere, or cheer them on at an event because he can't see them. Rough terrain walks are a no-go; he sleeps most often just when we start to get into deep discussion; he doesn't 'get' the boys on so many levels. We know he loves us all, and we love him, but it doesn't take away how hard the realities of this kind of living are. We are constantly looking for ways to honour him and find any activities we can all do together. I suggest you do that too and don't give up trying to find areas of connection.

Some things we have been able to adapt to as we have gone along. As my husband's eyes have deteriorated, we have moved to family quizzes that the boys read out instead of playing board or card games that he can't see. As his legs have got weaker, we have moved from long walks to short walks, from holidaying wherever and doing a whole manner of things to staying just in hotels and doing short family activities within a 20-minute walk or within driving distance for just one driver. There will perhaps come a point when we shall move to addressing wheelchair access and hoisting issues. Needless to say, the home educating and running of the household rests on my shoulders. For you, if there are two fully functioning parents then all the better, but just one will do, and even just part of one is sufficient if you can work out how to get a little extra help where needed.

The upshot is – and will be the same for any difference in your family – find, accept and focus on what you *can* do, and seek to enjoy life within those boundaries. It's much easier on the mind, spirit, body and emotions this way!

The most dramatic transformation has happened in me over the last few years, as I have let go of my previous expectations of what family life could have been for us. I desperately wanted a typical husband for me, and a dad for the boys, but when I now see what a blessing home education has been to my boys' character and faith, and how 'well' they've turned out regardless, I'm so relieved and thankful. That daily renewing of my mind for what God wants, and is in control of, has brought me through to a place of thankfulness and rest. That's not to say I don't occasionally slip back into being annoyed or discouraged because of the circumstances, but those moments are much fewer and farther between as the years go on.

There were many years that I prayed for my husband's healing and for him to change. Then there were many years that I prayed for me to change. Then, eventually, my prayers changed to prayers of thankfulness and for wisdom, to help me see the blessings and to help me *be* a blessing in my circumstances, and to allow the healing to take place in God's own time and in His own way. I wonder where you are on this journey as you read this today?

## Navigating the struggles

If your family isn't typical, then I'm assuming that your emotions and struggles are, by default, on another level. Maybe your child has a deteriorating condition; maybe they developed 'normally' for a while and then things started changing. Maybe you're grieving for the life you dreamed of, but which now never will be; maybe there's disappointment; maybe there's doubt, discouragement, fear, anger, or probably a combination of them all. Maybe you're wondering whether you should follow up the gut reaction that you know something's just a bit odd with one of your children but haven't taken it any further. There are lots of emotions and struggles we are taken through, in and through our life experiences, but I hope this chapter will speak truth, hope, and encouragement to bless you and help you on your way.

Having a child with a disability or difference – your biological own or adopted – will make you different no matter how much you have fitted in in the past, and no matter how much you've been able to enjoy life up until this point. The reality is that now you *are* different, and your life expectations *must* change. No disability, dysfunction or disorder is fun. But we can find joy in the smallest things. I don't like the 'dys / dis' in any of the above terms, but it can be helpful, nonetheless. The age-old question of whether to get a diagnosis or not will always be around; for some it will be the best thing to get one and for others the best thing not to pursue this. Just with home education and learning styles – each child and family is different – do what is right for you. Sometimes a diagnosis brings relief to them and you, a validation of your struggles, and access to services and therapies. Sometimes a diagnosis brings a label that some find restricting and best not to have.

Other 'typical' home-educating families perhaps get up, have devotions, have breakfast, work around the table, prepare lunch, do afternoon activities, come back, sit around the table for a meal, have bath time, books, games, TV and then bed. Typical parenting issues are relatively straightforward, but when you have a child with differences or when you, yourself or your spouse have challenges, all that normality is turned upside-down. Perhaps it's having a stressed household before breakfast because the clothes felt funny, or they can't pay attention to get themselves ready independently. Perhaps mealtimes are just the same five foods, or one meal is cooked for the family and there's another meal cooked for the child who is different. Perhaps it's that the children can't be home-educated in the same room because one makes too much noise or is too fidgety, so they have to work somewhere else. Perhaps it's frustration with not being able to read, or that handwriting is a battle. Maybe you can't go out and mix because having too much social interaction easily tips one child into a meltdown and he's crying and screaming and kicking and shouting, so social outings are limited, and the other siblings suffer as a result.

It's very easy to feel like a failure with any of the above – and they are just a few examples. If this touches on your life, then I suspect you could fill up this whole chapter with your particular story. Thankfully, just because something is hard, doesn't mean that it's wrong. It's just hard! Exhausting, maybe, yes. Tears may come daily, yes. But your love for your family and dedication will feed into them in ways that are profound and can give them an inner security that they are loved and valuable – whether you see that played out or reflected back yet or not.

It can also often feel like you're on your own, because no-one is actually there on the inside of your house to help, and on top of that, it's easy to be (or feel) judged. It is sad to say, but the sooner you can come to terms with the fact that you *will* be judged (and misjudged) for your actions and decisions, for what you do and how you do it, the better it will be for you. You will come to feel a lot of freedom and love to do what you know is best for your family without being dependent on others' good opinion of you. If it's your child that is different, then it's often you that is seen as the problem, and even the controlling and dominating one, because you have to say no to circumstances and situations which you know will have a detrimental impact on your child. You are not trying to be difficult – you want the opposite, but you are just trying to protect and do the best for your whole family.

It's very easy to be misunderstood, and when people misinterpret you, you have to deal with the emotional impact of that just as much as the difficulties of the reality of your life. There are many stresses and strains that you have to live with because many just don't understand.

But some do.

We don't need the whole world to be on our side – we just need to know that there are others out there who 'get it'. We may not be many, but we are not alone. Just like Elijah: he felt as though he was the only one, but that wasn't the truth. He may have felt like it was the truth, but thankfully, it still wasn't the truth.

As an occupational therapist (OT), founder of *www.chots.co.uk* (an online support for Christians around the world dealing with sensory and OT needs), *www.sensoryprocessing.co.uk* (for those who do not identify as Christians) and *www.occupationaltherapyjersey.com* (for those living in Jersey), I have come alongside families for years aiming to help support them and walk their journey with them. I have written a full book, 'Home Educating a Sensory Child – with Ease', and have online support and courses to help with the realities and the practical outworking of living with a child with OT and sensory needs on the autistic spectrum, ADHD, DCD, SPD, etc. There is not space to expand on that book in this chapter – I just want to emphasise that you are not alone, we do hear you and we are here for you.

**When the rubber hits the road**

Perhaps the hardest aspect of living differently is the constant giving when you get nothing in return, or when, "I hate you", or kicking, pinching, screaming, hitting, lack of sleep, or emotional withdrawal is your only reward. Very little strikes harder than this. For me as a Christian, it calls for deep intervention from the Holy Spirit in order to be able to take it and still respond in a Christlike manner.

For the most part, if they are giving you a hard time, it's because they are having a hard time. Oh, how we need all the wisdom and discernment we can get to really see what's at the root of it all, how to handle it well, and parent, and be in marriage, because that's what we do, and who we are, rather than because of what we get from it. It's the ultimate sacrifice and act of love.

As an aside – if you are being beaten or abused by the behaviours, then I would suggest you go for help, and that you remove yourself (or them) from that situation, but in most other circumstances it is our challenge to have that mind of Christ, and of Paul: to be content in all circumstances. That is my prayer for you as you read this.

**Final words of advice**

So, if I may offer some final words of advice:

Accept your child for who they are. Don't even try to conform to anyone else's way or any other family's way of being.

Adapt your curriculum to your child's needs.

Revise and adapt your life and schooling goals to what your child can realistically achieve, and celebrate each of those successes – no matter how small they may seem to you.

Take a good look at your hopes and dreams – write down the things you hoped for, the things you'll miss. Allow yourself to grieve and come to accept that those things may not happen – and ask yourself if you can live with that – and let them go.

Write down things to be thankful for, and blessings you have received – the internet, understanding friends, food to eat, shelter, air to breathe, safety, therapists, doctors, a health service – find and see the good bits in everything.

You may feel let down by others; if you have faith in God, write down who they are, and pray and tell God as you go down the list that you release them to Jesus and forgive them. It is your decision that will release you, not your emotions.

Come to accept that you are different, praying it aloud if you can (e.g. "Lord, we're different – and I'm alright with that") – and keep saying it until it moves from your head to your heart. Replace the word 'different' with whatever your struggle is.

Be faithful with what you have and who you are. Just like the boy in the Gospels who gave his few loaves and fishes to Jesus, who then multiplied them to feed thousands, give the little that you feel you are and can do to God, and see what He does.

Trust.

Do the best with who you are and what you've got.

You can do this. Accept that you will make mistakes – but that's alright. Do it perfectly imperfect.

Relax, and try and enjoy your journey. Your family is uniquely and wonderfully made. The only destination worth getting to is heaven, so there's no hurry.

Be thankful in everything.

Find out who God says you are and speak these truths over yourself to replace the negative talk and criticisms that come from others or yourself.

Keep communication lines open with your household – perhaps schedule a regular family chat time – to say thanks to them, to say what's bugging you about them, to ask for forgiveness, to work out solutions to a problem and so on.

Seek to honour one another.

Say sorry readily.

Remind yourself that a bad day at home is rarely as bad as a bad day at school.

Find help. It's alright – you should find help if you're feeling overwhelmed.

Allow space and time within your day to adapt to and go with the flow of special needs.

And finally, make room for the disability, difference, disorder or difficulty, to enjoy your home-educating journey as much as possible!

PART 2

# FIRM FOUNDATIONS THROUGH THE GENERATIONS

CHAPTER SIX

# HOME EDUCATION: IS IT FOR DADS TOO?

*Charles and Ruth Barber*

**The gift of parenthood**

When Ruth and I decided to home-educate our children, our eldest were twins aged 2½. They had been attending a playgroup for three mornings a week, run by a local church on an inner-city housing estate. Many of the children there had difficult backgrounds and the nursery was working hard to nurture them and improve their behaviour. Our experience, however, was the reverse! Each time our children came home it seemed they had picked up some more bad behaviour.

We decided to take the twins out of playgroup and have them entirely at home from their third birthday. In preparation for this, Ruth started to do a learning time on the mornings they were not going to playgroup. She organised activities including colouring, stories, cutting things out, learning the shape of letters, etc. She found it really hard work and the children were not particularly engaged or interested. She wondered how we would get on when we were doing this every day.

But on their first day at home, the children, as young as they were, somehow knew that today was different. When Ruth went into the dining room to start learning time, she was amazed to find both twins sat at the table, ready and waiting. For the whole of the morning the children participated eagerly and enthusiastically, asking questions and being fully engaged. The change was incredible!

Ruth had learnt the first of many lessons we were to learn on our home education journey: that when you send children to school or playgroup, you are unwittingly giving away a wonderful gift that rightly belongs to you as parents. You are effectively saying, 'This is where you go to learn, and these are the people who are going to teach you'. And in doing so, you are giving away a privilege and a responsibility that is yours. We believe it is the dad and mum who most naturally instruct and teach their children and have the child's interests most at heart. On that first Monday morning she reclaimed this gift.

But what about dads? I think it is easy as a dad to feel your role is not very important, especially with younger children. It is Mum who often does most of the frontline work, and probably she will be doing the bulk of the teaching. In fact, as we shall see in this chapter, home-educating is an extremely demanding task for both parents. Your decision will be tested in many different ways and Mum will need the full support of Dad on this journey. You will both need to be committed to it. This chapter sets out ten ways in which dads can 'step up' when it comes to home education.

## 1. Make sure you have a vision

Often it is Mum who first catches the vision for home educating, but Dad takes more convincing. I was an exception to this and was committed to home education from the outset. We had been impressed by the home-educating families we had encountered – how much the children seemed to know and how well brought up they seemed to be. I was excited about taking ownership of what my children would be learning and how they would be learning it. I decided they needed to learn Latin and they needed to know all the states of America before they were 5! I wanted them to learn English history properly. I planned for us to have long holidays in France so they could learn to speak French fluently. I wanted the boys to be able to climb trees and build dens, and the girls to wear dresses when they wanted. I wanted them to be taught not to use bad language, to be free from the way children are put down by their peers and their teachers and instead be secure and confident. And I wanted them to be able to pursue the things they were interested in. I had a vision and I wanted to be involved.

Over the years our understanding of and our reasons for home educating have grown and developed a great deal. Now I might set it out more like this:

- What is education? We live in a society that understands education to be primarily about gaining knowledge, developing academic and (to a lesser extent) sporting skills, and achieving success through exams, thereby finding employment. My wife and I believe that this is a very limited and product-centred approach to education. We would prefer to say that a 'proper' or rounded education or upbringing is about character, wisdom and (for us as Christians) the knowledge of God.

- Good character is about being polite, trustworthy, able to hold conversation, kind to one's friends, fun to be with, hard-working, and so on. It's about being the sort of person that other people want to befriend or have work for them.

- Wisdom is about being able to discern what is important in life – having your eyes open and not being taken in. It is about understanding what you can achieve and developing your potential. Learning and skills are part of wisdom, but not the whole.

- Knowledge of God is believing that this is His world and that certain things are fundamentally right or wrong. It also means recognising that each of us is created with our own gifts and talents that are important and needed, that we are loved and can be secure in ourselves, but also that the world does not revolve around us.

- Having a vision like this in the background has helped us to decide what is important day to day in home educating. It has put maths or reading skills into context and helped us not to feel inadequate when tempted to compare our children's education with what they would have been learning at school. I found it was often my role as Dad to bring us back to the vision and remind us of why we were home educating.

*2. Don't panic! Look for a way and you will find one*

Home education is a process of learning, step by step and day by day. We often got stuck and felt like giving up, especially Ruth, who bore the brunt of difficult days when I was out at work. My job here was to be level-headed, to keep calm and think things through, and to encourage Ruth when she wondered if we were achieving anything. The fact that we were struggling was often a sign that something needed to change. But each time we sat down and talked together, we found the next step, the next part of the jigsaw, the next idea that we needed to put into place. But we didn't start out knowing all the answers; we just had a shared vision and a mutual commitment to the journey.

At the same time, we appreciated lots of encouragement and ideas from other families, especially through an annual holiday for Christian home-educating families that we started to attend each year. It was helpful to talk to other parents and find that many of our struggles were common.

One of my early worries was how I was going to be able to give our children a chance to learn to play sports when I was so very un-sporty myself! But the worry turned out to be unnecessary. They started playing with friends and neighbours in the garden and learnt to swim and play table tennis on campsites in France. Then they got involved in local clubs playing cricket and hockey. They have now played significant roles in various teams in hockey, cricket and table tennis, as well as enjoying football, swimming, golf, cycling and running!

### 3. *Discipline your children appropriately*

Squabbles between siblings are the norm of family life, especially when you are living in a relatively confined space, 24/7. It is tempting to just try and prevent them and keep the home as peaceful as possible, but underneath the squabbles there are often real issues that need to be faced. Once, following a particularly traumatic few days, Ruth believed that God spoke to her through a picture of a rainbow. Like the different colours, our children all have different personalities. This can cause conflict as individual characters rub up against each other and we shouldn't feel too concerned about it. As we work at it, we can learn to live together and come to appreciate the differences in each other.

We wanted our children to learn to deal with squabbles by putting things right. This was done by having an honest reflection of what each one had done wrong and then each saying, "I'm sorry" and "I forgive you". We were strict about them resolving conflicts before they moved onto other things.

We were tested, of course, by our own teaching! When I lost my temper and started shouting at one of my children, I had to begin the discipline process by saying sorry for what I had done wrong. This did not undermine the discipline, but rather made it real and modelled the desired response.

Mums need the support of their husbands in disciplining children. It is not so much about, 'Wait until your father gets home'. It is just that the children need to know that you as parents are agreed on what is wrong and what the consequences will be. And a lack of discipline can leave children insecure as well as unruly.

Another revelation we had was about the difference between teaching and training. Teaching your children that certain things are wrong (and why) is very important. Showing them that good character has positive effects, for them as well as others, should instil in them a desire to do what is good. But children require training as well. They need to be challenged and disciplined when they do the wrong thing, and practise doing the right thing. Like shutting the door again instead of slamming it, or asking again in the right way.

I think with all of our seven children, we have gone through a time of crisis, a difficult period, when we had to pray and think and work hard. I remember sitting on the floor in an airport whilst Sam, aged 3, was having a tantrum. He yelled and yelled. I was waiting for the security guards to come. All the world seemed to be passing by and watching us. This tantrum period seemed to go on a long time, certainly months. There was no easy answer. We just had to be patient, and firm, trying to work through to the roots of the problem. Eventually they stopped happening. Manny, our number five, was the most placid of our children. He was very independent and easy to look after. But about the age of 6 he met with some discipline he didn't like. Storming upstairs and slamming doors all started in earnest, and we had to try to understand the roots of his anger and how to cope with it.

### 4. Protect your children's natural inquisitiveness and freedom to learn

Home education starts with the basic premise that children have a natural inclination to learn and be creative. So, it is natural for young children to want to grub about and look at insects, or make dens out of branches, or tie things together with string, or stick them with glue, or dress up, or paint, or ...

If school is guilty of one thing above many, it is that it knocks children's creativity and inquisitiveness out of them by telling them what to learn and when to learn it, what to do and what to be interested in, rather than allowing them to explore and discover the world for themselves.

I remember our son Sam eagerly wanting me to get on his bed and read to him about the Hundred Years War. I re-learnt the Battle of Agincourt when he was about 7. When we went to Dinan on a family holiday, he recognised a statue of Bertrand du Guesclin (1340-80) in the car park. He knew who it was and what he was famous for. I was completely dismissive and told him it could be anyone. But he was insistent, and when we went over to look at the plaque, he was right! I had never even heard of the man.

When our daughter Beth was 9, she read 'Villette' by Charlotte Brontë. Ruth had also recently read the book and found the language and long sentences quite hard going, so she was sceptical of Beth's claim to have read it. Ruth asked her to tell her what it was about, and Beth relayed the plot in detail. At about the same time I was doing my bit by teaching Beth to tell the time from a clock. I spent two weeks going over exercises with her to explain what the two hands meant, and at the end of it I gave up. I resolved to let her work out how to tell the time when she was ready. Sometime between then and now (she is 21) she has managed to do so.

Home education is about working with the child's natural creativity, allowing their unique personality and interests to develop, giving them opportunity to discover, and learning with them. It's easy to spend so much time worrying about curriculum styles and learning resources that you limit the child's ability to learn naturally.

Within the contemporary ecological concept of re-wilding, home education is about rediscovering how children naturally grow up, how they naturally learn and how God intended family to work and to be. It is letting go of tightly held control over what happens day to day, the defined and limited outcomes of traditional education, and the productivity-centred approach of school that measures progress by looking at a few particular indicators. It is allowing the natural features of family life to develop unfettered, such as having a meal together, going for walks together, keeping relationships right and loving each other, confronting issues without imposing quick-fix solutions.

Once, when Ruth was obviously having a difficult day, one of our well-meaning friends said, "Why don't you just put them into school?" – as if this would deal with all the issues of growing up as a family.

5. *Help your children to acquire the self-discipline they need to learn for themselves*

We would say that home education does not aim to impart knowledge *per se*, but aims to help the child acquire the skills needed to learn. Then they can learn anything! As parents, this became clearer to us over time. Part of our thinking was formed by considering the classical trivium of logic, language and rhetoric. The ancient civilisations saw learning as not just about learning facts or basic principles (logic), but about being able to use those facts to gain understanding of and talk about the world (language), and then to think for oneself, argue a case, or present a point of view (rhetoric).

A friend of ours made a short video about how being home-educated helped him to acquire the skills needed to learn. When he went to college to study A Levels he engaged enthusiastically with his lessons and when he didn't know something he went and found out the answer for himself. One of his teachers was so impressed with his attitude that he asked him which school he had attended, because he wanted to send his own children there! School does not generally teach children those skills. It concentrates on imparting knowledge and exam technique.

Acquiring these skills does however involve the discipline of study, and includes reading, maths, learning information, understanding ideas, and so on. It requires the self-discipline to learn stuff that you are not immediately interested in because it will give you the tools needed to find out more about things you are interested in later on. And whilst there are endless approaches to curricula amongst home-educating families, we finally decided to teach our children towards GCSEs and A Levels. Nevertheless, the way they learnt was very different to school, as it was done mostly from books and with very little direct teaching or instructing from us. We have taken a tutoring style approach where I would set them work from a coursebook and go through it with them periodically or anytime when they needed help. They have learned to carry the responsibility for their own learning.

One of our growing realisations as a home-educating family was that every family is unique, and this is how it is supposed to be. This is about Mum and Dad, their personalities, interests and skills, as well as about the children themselves. In other words, education does not come out of a box or even a book – it has to be discovered. I found that conversations with other families, and on my part with other dads, have been essential, not just for giving us ideas on how we could do things, but also for helping us define how we are different to them.

## 6. Take responsibility for what your children are learning

We also came to realise that we were responsible for everything our children were learning, not just what we were teaching them. What would they learn from the TV, from books, from peers, and later from the internet? We made an early decision that we would not have a TV, simply because there was so much on it that we were unhappy with. We didn't want to be overprotective. We knew they had to be prepared to live in the real world. But we wanted to prepare them, to teach them to be critical and recognise deceit. So, instead of TV we watched carefully selected films or cartoons together as a family.

It was the same with books. Ruth tried to read or part-read all books before the children read them, though this eventually became impossible. Trips to the library resulted in huge stacks of books that they wanted to borrow, which we then carefully sifted. We were regularly horrified at some of the content that children / young adults were exposed to in these books. We took time to show them some of the reasons for our decisions and, as they got older, taught them how to decide what to read for themselves.

We were also concerned about the sexual content of many books, films, songs and websites. We intended that our children would not be exposed to sexual ideas until they were older, and then it would be from a perspective of marriage and courtship rather than teenage 'relationships'. In the Bible, the Song of Songs says there is a right time to "awaken love" (2:7). We wanted to encourage our children to develop good strong friendships with both sexes from which genuine relationships might come in time.

Generally, I think that parents, and dads in particular, take little responsibility for what their children are learning and just allow society to dictate. In the Bible we read, "Listen, my son, to your father's instruction and do not forsake your mother's teaching" (Proverbs 1:8). To me, that means that dads have a responsibility.

### 7. *Help Mum develop a structure to the day that works*

I don't think it is possible to have your children with you all day and every day, and enjoy it (!), without having some firm structures in place. Family discipline is not an option or an extra; it is an essential requirement to survival.

When our children were young, we started each day with a family praise time to put God at the centre of the day. As they got older, we taught them to start each day with a time of individual Bible reading. We also required our children to share in daily chores because it was good for them to learn household skills, and we developed a rota for their daily jobs. We also expected them to help with meal preparation. Familiarity with the kitchen has helped all of them to learn to bake cakes, scones and biscuits, and prepare proper meals.

Another part of our daily routine was having a post-lunch quiet time for everybody, which would give Ruth a break. Young ones might be still having a rest, but the older ones had to find an activity to do on their own, and do quietly – in principle for an hour, but often lasting a couple of hours. This had to be something they could do unsupervised. It might be reading but could also be playing with Lego, or cutting out and making things. We believed it was a good habit for all our children to learn to be self-occupied and decide for themselves what they were going to do. Computers and media were not allowed during this time.

For the first few years Ruth planned something in which all our children could engage at different levels, perhaps based round a story or a particular morning activity. Sometimes they would go out to meet other families at a bird sanctuary, park or museum. As they got older, joint activities became more difficult and one of our early crises was having to re-think our daily routine. This resulted in our introducing a morning timetable for each child, allowing the older ones to do schoolwork based around books, whilst the younger ones could focus more on craft or play activities with a sibling. Ruth needed to know what everyone was going to do, at least in principle, before the morning started.

In hindsight, the need for occasional modifications to routine seems obvious and straightforward, but when you are struggling with a family and finding the day is not working, deciding what to do can seem very daunting. We needed to be able to sit down together, consider options, think outside the box and sometimes try different things before we knew what would work.

*8. Make sure your children feel loved and listened to, and encourage them to be sociable*

When we had our fourth child, we decided he should be called Isaac, knowing that the meaning of the name is 'laughter'. We couldn't have been more spot on, as Isaac turned out to have a very infectious giggle from an early age which was quite different to any of the others. His cheeky smile was made more endearing because of notable dimples in his cheeks. Isaac was also the most affectionate of our children and, when people came to visit, within just a few minutes he was sat next to them or on their knee, peering at a book he had brought to show them. He was naturally outgoing and normally the first to make friends with other children when we were on holiday – his siblings would push him forward and follow closely behind.

One of the biggest misconceptions about home education is that home-taught children lack the social skills that other children learn at school, or indeed that school actually helps children to socialise. We firmly believe the opposite – that school typically de-skills children from socialising, whether with their peers, with adults or with younger children. How often have I, like you probably, walked up the street when teenage children are coming home from school. If you dare to engage with them by saying hello or nodding your head, the response is often a blank look or a sneer of disinterest. It is not 'cool' to engage with adults because teenagers see adults as quasi-teachers.

It is not cool to talk to younger children, because they do not engage at your sophisticated level. And it is only cool to talk with your peers about certain 'in' topics, rather than about the real issues of life. I may exaggerate, but I am sure this sounds familiar.

Socialising with other people is one of the most natural of instincts. But the foundation of all social interaction is a sense of self-worth which we would say comes from knowing that God made you and loves you. This self-worth gives us the confidence to engage openly, trustingly, and meaningfully with others. To look people in the eye. To start a conversation. To introduce ourselves. People do not need to be taught to socialise, though they may need to be taught the finer arts of social engagement in terms of manners and politeness.

But if self-worth is knocked out of a person, then their confidence to engage goes and people hide behind a front that they feel is acceptable, to protect themselves from being hurt further. They look away or down at the ground, or they put on an over-confident, false front. When I was at school, I was teased about just about everything and it left me shy, retiring, rude, defensive, jealous and distant from others. As a teenager, I found talking with adults difficult, even when I wanted to.

When our children were still small, we attended a holiday for Christian home-educating families, and I remember being introduced to a young man who was about 17. Instead of struggling through an awkward conversation (which was my expectation), the young man engaged with me confidently and openly, asking me about myself, my family, how the holiday was going, and telling me about himself and what he was doing with his life. It was a truly pleasant conversation, and if either of us found it difficult, it was me.

Our experience has been that home-educated families normally produce very sociable children. We have often been to events where we just threw our children into the mix and they were playing happily with other children they had never met before within minutes. Generally, they are not shy, age-conscious, apprehensive about how other children will receive them, inclined to gang behaviour, unnatural with the opposite sex, or any of the other things that impede normal social interaction. Of course, home-educated children will vary in personality, like all children. If Isaac was our most naturally outgoing, then Joe, our number three, was the most naturally shy and retiring. But within the context of family, his musical and technical abilities and sense of humour have all flourished and been valued.

Equally, our children have played easily with neighbours' children, even though we live in a very sociologically and ethnically mixed area. They have come to the fore in organising games of football, or working out how to deal with fallouts, or making sure that everyone is included. The problem has been that we have had to draw the line at how much social engagement they are having with neighbours' children when bad behaviour or language has entered our home as a result. And you have to teach your children to not trust everybody, but to be "wise as serpents and innocent as doves" (Matthew 10:16).

The norm for home-educated children is family, and they naturally relate to other people as distant family members. They learn to treat others with respect and expect to be respected themselves. They learn to care for younger siblings, to learn from older ones, to be polite to adults, to talk and to be included. They answer the door, offer drinks, make conversation, show interest, and ask people to play with or be interested in them. They are quick to make friends, organise games and tell stories. They don't judge you or disapprove of you. This was driven home to us when some friends, whose boys go to school, came round to visit. The boys said afterwards the reason they enjoyed coming to visit us was *because they were treated like family.*

### 9. *Know your values and impart them to your children*

For us as a Christian family, making Sunday special (including not playing sport), teaching our children to trust God and to pray, and developing good characters were key parts of our education journey. Some people say children should be allowed to choose. Well, of course children will choose in time, as they grow older, but when they are young, they are extremely impressionable – if they are not shaped by parents, they will be shaped by their exposure to wider society. And it is naïve to think we live in a society that is impartial about matters of faith and morality. Modern education theory has a very clear agenda of teaching children that traditional Judeo-Christian values of family life are outdated or even harmful to the progress of the modern world, and encouraging lifestyle choices that Bible-believing Christians would disagree with.

Having said that, church can be one of the biggest hurdles for home-educating families because most churches are structured (like the rest of society) on a school model: one person at the front and everyone else sat listening. It can be very boring and does not create strong, thinking followers. The other aspect of school is that you separate people into age or development groupings and only learn with your peers.

The family model, in contrast, is everyone sat around the table. It includes all ages and expects everyone to participate. Dad, at the head of the table, neither knows everything nor does all the talking. He is just Dad, which gives him authority and leadership, which he uses to encourage others to participate, ask questions and contribute to conversation. In this way all the members of the family learn and grow together. Interestingly, the best sort of workforce training involves interaction, role play and discussion, with only a limited amount of 'instruction' from the trainer.

We have tried to apply the family model to all of our learning. Like many Christian home-educating families, we felt we needed to do 'church' on our own for a number of years to enable our children to fully participate. This gave us time as a family to address character issues, apply our faith to real everyday situations, and grow in our understanding together.

As a family we are now part of a local church again, where we do our part to encourage everyone to participate, share ideas and stories, and engage in the worship. But we still consider us as parents, and me in particular as Dad, to have the responsibility for bringing up our children in the ways of God. It is not the responsibility of the pastor, or the youth leader, or the Sunday School teacher, to teach and train our children about following Jesus.

*10. Help your children to become independent, responsible adults*

Young adulthood starts when children are about 12 or 13. This is when they start to assert their independence and begin to form their own ideas or understanding, that may not be quite the same as yours. Room needs to be made for their particular skills and interests. Sam wanted to play for a good hockey club with a national side. I had to help find one and then take him there to train. Our boys wanted to join a table tennis club. They went onto the internet and found one, and we joined as a family. Beth missed the connection with other girl friends from home-educating families. She started by writing letters and later began to chat to friends online. We organised sleepovers for her.

At the age of 12, Jesus was taken by His parents to Jerusalem for the feast, but on their return, they found they had lost Him. After three days of searching, they found Him sitting in the Temple courts debating with the Jewish teachers – yet His father was a carpenter! When they scolded Him, Jesus replied, "Why didn't you know where I would be?" (Luke 2:49). This was their wake-up call. Children grow up. And so they should.

Young adulthood is the time when you don't just tell your children what to do, but you discuss things with them and start to give them responsibility for their decisions, even when they get it wrong. You start to listen to them, debate with them and nurture them into adulthood. You wait more for them to ask you for advice, rather than insisting on them doing things your way.

Parents only have a caretaker role, and that for a relatively short number of years. Ultimately, all good parenting aims at letting children grow into mature adults who are free and able to pursue their own vision, with a confidence drawn from their secure upbringing. There is nothing more stifling than a father who tries to live out his disappointments through his children or a mother who clings to her children out of her own self-need and insecurity. The goal is to finish your parenting role with a strong, trusting relationship with your adult offspring.

I am proud of our children, in a humble sort of way. They are not clones, either of us or of the state system. They are each finding their own place in the world. And I am confident you would love to meet them!

**Stepping up**

There is a quote from the Bible which is about John the Baptist, who came to prepare people for Jesus. "He will turn the hearts of the fathers to their children and the hearts of children to their fathers, lest I come and smite the land with a curse" (Malachi 4:6, RSV). In a day in which manhood is diminished as never before, dads need to rise up to their God-given role of preparing their children to live lives that make a difference in this world. A generation who are confident, secure, not put down but firm in their convictions, courteous, loving, outgoing, gentle. Such people are formed, in part, by having dads who love them from the heart, and have time to teach and train them into adulthood. This is our privilege and responsibility. Let us reclaim what belongs to us.

CHAPTER SEVEN

# HELP! MY GRANDCHILDREN ARE BEING HOME-EDUCATED: HOME EDUCATION AND THE WIDER FAMILY

*Helen Brunning*

As I write this chapter, three of my children's cousins are staying with us for our annual 'Cousin Camp'. They will explore the woods together, compete in the 'Cousin Camp Cook Off', make a new film and enjoy each other's company. They'll learn about what unites them as cousins as well as what differences there are across the family. It's a great week of hilarity, noise, collaboration, arguments – resolutions – and memory-making.

I have always been very keen to involve our wider family, and especially grandparents, in the education of our children: both in their formal learning and in the wider life learning that is so important for the development of rounded young people.

The first part of this chapter looks at some concerns the wider family might have about the home education journey; the second part looks at some of the ways in which family members can be included in it.

**Concerns from the wider family**

When parents start contemplating home educating their children, their wider family members can have a variety of different reactions. Even if they are broadly sympathetic, they may still express concerns. Four common concerns are outlined briefly here.

*Concern 1 – The children will not have any friends*

Lots of grandparents have an initial worry that home education will isolate their grandchildren. As soon as you get involved in the world of home education, though, you quickly see that this is not the case. Home educators get to help their children with making lifelong, meaningful friendships, as well as with learning to socialise with anyone and everyone who comes their way. The 2-year-old who lives next door, the 12-year-old who also enjoys cycling – but also the librarian, the road mender, the shop assistant. Children can start early in building real-life, real-world relationships.

There are always children who find it harder to make friends – you will find them amongst school-educated as well as home-educated children. In my experience, home-educated children have a greater capacity to pursue their own unique interests, which can then help them make connections with a wide selection of people with whom they have something in common.

My children have made life-long friendships with other children in our home education group. And, of course, there are also friends from their Scouts and Guides, music groups, church and our local neighbourhood.

*Concern 2 – The children's parents will miss out*

There is sacrifice involved in becoming a home-educating parent. You may have to give up or adapt some of the plans you had before. I was once interviewed about home education. "What is the best part of home education?" asked the interviewer. "Being with my children 24/7", I replied. "I love being with them as they discover new things about their world and it's great to guide them through their learning journey." "And what is the hardest part of home education?" "Being with my children 24/7!", I quipped.

Of course, the truth is that you are not with your children 24/7. As they grow and develop, they spread their wings in their own time and have more and more capacity for sorting themselves out.

That being said, most home-educating parents will tell you that with the sacrifices comes great joy. Their life plans are not necessarily derailed, though perhaps they are shifted in an unexpected direction. The home education world as a whole can benefit from the range of experiences that different parents bring with them. I have found an outlet for many of my interests and abilities within the home education community.

There can also be a financial impact, although this can often be overcome or at least mitigated. In our family, my husband is the main breadwinner, but I also have a small part-time paid job. Other home-educating parents share the education of the children while both also work part-time. Still others manage to set up a business from home, and this brings with it its own opportunities for the children to learn excellent life lessons.

*Concern 3 – The children will be behind*

When your child arrives, you are flooded with pieces of advice, the most oft repeated of which I can remember is, "Don't compare". Whether your child eats, crawls, walks or talks first or last in the group, you are told not to worry. Aside from concerns that need specific attention, parents are told repeatedly that their children will each learn these basic things in their own time, and that that is fine. Why, then, should it be any different when it comes to learning to read, write and learn about their world? Who is measuring, and why? Who will the child be 'behind' – indeed who will they be 'ahead of'?

And as for those specific concerns – the children with extra learning or physical needs – how marvellous to be in their own home environment and grow at their own pace, without a daily comparison that tells them they aren't up to scratch yet.

When I began home educating, I had to learn this for myself. "I'm totally up for the premise that my child will learn to read when he is ready", I used to muse. "I just wish he was ready at 4½ when everyone else is supposed to be!" I gritted my teeth and waited and, sure enough, when he was ready to read it came very quickly and he soon had his nose stuck almost permanently in a book. Except when it was stuck in his pile of Lego! With the benefit of glorious hindsight, I look back and think that if I had pushed him to read when he was 'supposed' to, it would have taken longer, been more stressful and left him with a dislike of reading.

The same applies to older children too. If they are learning because they want to, are ready to or need to (to get somewhere else they want to be), the learning is smoother and more readily entered into. You might just have to hold your breath a bit!

*Concern 4 – The children will be unusual*

Every person is a unique and marvellous individual. Everyone has different interests, needs, mannerisms. All of these make up the parts that are specific to you and no-one else. It's a great privilege to help raise children who are confident in their own skin, who are able to be themselves.

I am delighted that my children are not like anyone else! I am excited by their individualities. They are all different to each other, as well as to me and my husband.

**How to deal with these concerns**

If you are home-educating and your wider family expresses some or all of these concerns to you, how do you cope? First and foremost, remember that the education and upbringing of your children is your decision. There are many times when your family may have different ideas from you, for all sorts of reasons. And they can be expressed in many ways, from gentle worry to forceful antagonism. Hopefully, you can encourage them to read this chapter – and the rest of this book – to help them come to grips with this new idea in their lives. But ultimately there may come a time when you need to firmly thank them for their concern and leave it at that.

When we decided to educate our eldest at home, we wondered how our families might feel. We wrote them a letter setting out some of our reasons – and explicitly stating that it was in no way a comment on the way we had been educated! We also said that we were only planning to educate at home for the first three years and, even then, would reconsider the situation carefully each year. When we got to the end of those three years, there was another letter! Now that we had seen how well things were working out for us and had made so many great home education connections, we would continue for the foreseeable future. The point is that by promising to evaluate yearly, we lessened any concern there might have been, instead of just saying, "Hey! We're going to do this strange thing to your grandchildren for the next 14 years!" By the time the second letter arrived on their doorsteps, they were already seeing the fruits of this educational choice and could see that the children were happy and thriving.

**Involving the wider family**

The beauty of home education is being able to shape it exactly the way you want. This means you can bring other people into your child's and family's life on the basis you feel will most add meaning. In this section I share some of the ways that you may like to consider involving your family.

First, though, I realise that some reading this book may not have much of a wider family that they can call on. How can these tips help them? I highly recommend building your own 'family' around you: good friends, fellow churchgoers, other home educators near and far. People you can trust to encourage you and your children, and who can play the role of 'grandparent', 'aunt' or 'cousin' in your child's life when their own are not available for various reasons.

My children's grandparents are not too far away, but not close enough for a weekly pop-in. For a time, I enlisted an older member of the church for each of the eldest two. This was an adult who was interested in them, spent time with them and included them in activities such as they might have done with their grandparents had they been closer. Similarly, some of my good friends have become extra 'uncles' and 'aunts' to my children. I have always appreciated the fact that my children can hear other adult voices speaking into their lives, bringing a slightly different perspective on things that matter.

You may feel you have to step out of your comfort zone a little to create this wider family. But I really encourage you to find others – one family at a time – with whom you can share some time. I have seen many lovely friendships develop in home education circles where whole families have connected to great mutual benefit.

How, then can relatives play a part in the education of your children?

*Sharing knowledge*

Firstly, there can be the sharing of knowledge. If Uncle Dan is a carpenter – and if he is willing – he can be asked to share his knowledge with his niece or nephew. If he isn't able to help them create something, he can show them his work and talk about the process of creating. Spending time with someone with a talent will, at the very least, help children see how wide the world is, and how many opportunities there are to follow your interests and dreams.

My mother was a nurse and has always been fascinated by the study of the human body. One of her favourite books is full of all sorts of medical pictures that are really rather gruesome when you aren't as excited by the subject as she is! When my daughters wanted to learn biology, we bought Grandma a copy of the book they were using, and she had a weekly video call with them to guide them through each section. This brought a lot of life to their books as she was able to add her own stories from her nursing days to most pages.

Perhaps you have a relative who doesn't feel that they have a skill or knowledge they can share, but who would still like to gain a deeper relationship with your children. Just popping in for a chat can sometimes be difficult because some people struggle to cross the generation gap. Can they instead commit to reading aloud to the children? This can be done in person if they live close by, or across the phone or video calls if necessary. If they choose a book that is meaningful to them, they are passing on a bit of family history as well as connecting with the next generation. Once a week, or however often, relationships will be deepened, and memories will be made.

*A willing and sympathetic audience*

As much as the wider family can share knowledge with your children, they can also be fantastic recipients for the sharing of knowledge *by* your children. Any time a new skill is learned, what better audience to show this off to than the family around them? When they've learned to write, many relations will love receiving handwritten post. When they've learned a new ball skill, it can be shared with the grandparents. Live if possible, recorded if not!

As well as regular updates, how about combining a few and making a special event of it: a termly or yearly family 'revue' where everyone gets together and showcases a few things they've learned or perfected recently. This is ideal for showing new musical or dance skills and can also include a presentation about knowledge they've recently acquired. Practising towards a specific date gives a great focus to get skills polished up for an audience; the friendly faces keep the pressure off if anything does go awry. You know your own children and whether this pressure would be too much for them. You can assess how long they might need to become ready for such an event. And of course, preparing to present is itself a valuable lesson, which many of us need in our adult lives.

It is often said that teaching something is a good way to make sure you've learned it yourself. In the home education world, you can make the most of that by enabling your child to teach someone else the knowledge they have recently acquired. This is different to just showing something or presenting information. You can make it spontaneous or planned, depending on your child's ability and temperament. You can announce it yourself – "Katya's just learned some facts about Egypt. She'd really like to teach you what she knows"

– or prime your relation quietly to ask for it – "Aunt Renee, ask Eli to teach you about swans."

*Family history*

Your family's history is as much 'real' history as the World Wars or the first trip across the Atlantic. Every family has a wealth of stories and they come with special feeling and emotion that only the people who experienced them can pass on. If your family has a difficult or complicated history, you may want to tread carefully here and ensure that what is revealed to your child is appropriate. However, learning to be a young historian, geographer or researcher includes learning to gather information from sources – and what better sources than the people who were actually there, taking part in the event?

When we studied the first moon landing, my son was able to ring his Grandpa and ask him about the event, about what he remembered and how he felt about it. How did he hear about it in an age before the internet (something my son could only just imagine!)? Grandpa also kindly dug out the memorabilia he had kept from the time, which we all found interesting to see when we were next able to visit. There are other major world events which your family will remember and be able to talk about with your children, bringing them to life in a way that books just can't quite match.

Of course, national and international events aren't the only events that make a family history. One of my grandmothers lived in what was then Burma before the civil war. I often wish I had made time to ask her more about her daily life there, so different from anything I have known. Relatives can tell your children about all sorts of private events that have shaped your family and made it what it is today. You can assist your children in becoming investigators by planning questions to ask, and you can help them compare the answers from different generations or the different sides of your family. If your children have a heritage that reaches out beyond the country you now live in, this is a significant opportunity to help them understand their place in the world.

What is more, how exciting for your child to discover that what they did yesterday is now 'historic'! Their daily rhythms and routines are history for someone in the future. If they have smaller cousins, they can pass on their own 'family history' in some way. They can begin sentences with, "I remember when ...". They can pass on a funny story about themselves to amuse and be added to the family folklore.

My daughter loves the story about her and the sandwich. One evening when she was 3 years old, she told us she was still hungry very shortly after a decent dinner. We were surprised but asked if she wanted a sandwich. She agreed that she did. "OK", we said. "If we make you a sandwich, you must eat it." She agreed and the sandwich was produced. She wasn't hungry. She didn't want it. We left her at the table contemplating the unwanted sandwich with the admonition that she had asked for it, she had agreed to eat it and eat it she must. After several minutes of stand-off, her voice was heard, quite quietly, calling her elder brother. "Henry? Henry? Do you want a sandwich?" We had to chuckle at this new tactic! I can't remember what happened next, although she was allowed to leave the table soon after (I suspect the sandwich was wrapped up for breakfast) and we all laugh about it now. A piece of family history made, preserved and handed down.

*Encouraging through reluctance*

What your child might baulk at doing for you, they may be delighted to do for someone else in the family. Part of my style of home education includes getting my children to read aloud to me. We've had some lovely moments snuggled up on the sofa together. However, my youngest daughter was less enthusiastic about this than her elder siblings had been. I was disappointed that she lost this practice reading time until, ironically, Covid-19 came to my aid. When she heard of the fun and games her aunt was having with her own two youngsters home from school, my daughter asked if she could read to them by video call once a week. This was great for them – and for me! A weekly tradition was started which hasn't stopped yet. Read-aloud practice for my daughter, delight for her cousins, a deeper relationship across the family. Everyone wins!

This can also work with other areas of reluctance. If your children don't like writing for you, they might like to write letters or postcards to grandparents, or stories for their younger cousins. Last year our smaller cousins were given a book of ten original illustrated stories written by one of my daughters. Sometimes a reluctant writer needs a good reason to write and that can often come from the wider family.

*Occasional takeovers*

For some years, my part-time job had an annual full-day meeting I had to attend. It would have been possible for my husband to take the day off work, but instead we invited my parents to come and be 'substitute teachers' for the day. I would make a list of the books we were currently using and leave them to it. They would all have a great day together – Grandma and Grandad would be exhausted at the end of it! – and it provided our children with another perspective on learning and interest and different voices to listen to.

My children have also enjoyed the times when relatives have been around to take them to swimming, gymnastics or netball practice – especially when they stay and watch. Another opportunity for greater understanding of what's important to the children and what their week looks like.

*Being a blessing to each other*

The flexibility of home education means your children can learn from the ups and downs of life in the wider family. If a relative needs extra support for a time – after childbirth, or during illness, for example – the children can join with you in sharing blessing and assistance.

When my father was ill, we were able to take our books with us and stay at my parents' home whenever we needed to. The home education was able to continue around the life lessons being learned through encouraging and caring together.

Most years, our home education group has a Sports Day in a local park. This is a great opportunity to get together and have a lot of fun.

Many of the working parents book the afternoon off work so they can join us too and there is often a number of grandparents or other relatives joining in the merriment. One home-educating mum was particularly glad her parents were able to attend. Initially sceptical about home education, they had been gradually warming to the idea as they saw how fulfilled their grandchildren were. The Sports Day – with its range of children of all ages and abilities taking part together – really helped them to see what a good thing home education could be. They watched the teens (older than their eldest grandchild) happily joining in themselves or taking time to encourage the younger ones and could see with their own eyes evidence that further dispelled their worries. They were able to gain in confidence about the future ahead of their own, much-loved grandchildren.

Home education is a choice you make for your immediate family. If you are able to bring the wider family into it with you, there can be benefits all round in broader experiences, deep-rooted relationships and shared memories. In a world which is often ready to dismiss older people, you can buck the trend and help your children see that they can learn from previously won wisdom and experience. Meanwhile, older relatives can find themselves enjoying a new perspective on life from their younger kin. Home education really can be a journey that grows families.

CHAPTER EIGHT

# STANDING ON THE SHOULDERS OF GIANTS: THE VIEW FROM SECOND-GENERATION HOME EDUCATORS

*Philippa Nicholson*

I have never been to school. My only knowledge of what it might be like has been gained from listening to friends' experiences or living vicariously through literature and other accounts. Anne Shirley with her infamous broken slate, William Brown's 'Outlaws' and school masters, Laura Ingalls' one-room schoolhouse, Miss Wormwood's classroom in the Calvin and Hobbes cartoon strips, Tom Brown's experiences at Rugby. Incomplete and often outdated though they are, these stories all framed my childhood understanding of what school is like.

I will never actually know what it's like to sit daily in a classroom as a child and learn alongside a gaggle of children, all born within a few months of me. I have never struggled to make friends at playtime or felt lost in a crowded secondary school corridor.

Curious folk would ask if I minded 'missing out' on school, but how can a child compare two such different educational journeys when immersed in only one? Even as an adult, comparison of the two remains hypothetical, so that task is best left to those who have experienced both worlds.

**First-generation home education**

Home-educating families, as you likely already know from experience or from reading through this book, are as varied as humanity itself. Let me give you a glimpse of mine.

I'm the eldest of nine siblings – two girls and seven boys – and we were all home-educated by our parents, starting with me in the late 1980s. My mother had been a primary school teacher before I came along, and my father had a varied career which included multi-subject secondary school teaching in England and Africa. Having seen many different aspects of the school system, neither wanted to entrust their children to Godless institutions in which they could not guide and protect us.

On hearing of their teaching careers, curious folk who inquired about our lifestyle would often say that my parents were qualified to be home educators. After all, they were professional teachers! My mother always disagreed: being able to organise a class of children can actually be a hindrance when learning how to be a parent-educator. For a start, your own children simply can't be organised in the same way as a class of pupils from whom you can walk away at the end of a long day; expecting it to be similar at home can lead to a rude awakening.

My siblings and I had a freestyle education which centred on the core subjects of English and Maths yet with a relaxed approach in general. We never needed to take 'school' holidays as the pace of learning was so laidback that it looked horizontal much of the time. We were surrounded by books which, in the pre-internet age, were devoured in volume. Allowed to develop at our own pace, we were a mix of late and early readers who enjoyed a broad range of subjects from computer science to history. I remember plenty of time for open-ended garden play with space for our imaginations to flourish. Looking back, we had a 'Charlotte Mason' style of education (see also Appendix A) but with the omission of the core tool of narration (Mason, e.g. 1886, p.233).

I accumulated a variety of O Levels, IGCSEs and other qualifications like Scout badges, from the age of 13. My mother would find an exam centre, source the syllabus and course books and then pretty much leave me to it. I was driven by the curiosity in the subject which had led me to choose it in the first place. Six months later, we would repeat the process again with a new subject.

By the time my younger batch of siblings hit secondary school, my parents had discovered Open University courses and my brothers started those instead of traditional exam routes. Most of us studied for undergraduate degrees while living at home, and some went on to masters and a PhD.

Many different styles of education can nurture a love of life-long learning. My parents facilitated my education in a way which fostered a wonder of God's world and a desire to learn which continues to this day.

**The next generation**

Educating my own children at home was always my long-term plan but, until they came along, I can't say that I analysed my educational experience. In the words of my sister, "You don't really examine *why* or *how* you can breathe, you just sort of get on with it." Education was certainly this way for me until my husband, Andy, and I had our first child and responsibility loomed.

Having come from a home in which the only stated educational philosophy was summarised as 'better late than early', as a young mother I threw myself into being a student of the different approaches to home education. Andy and I settled on the structure which we felt would best fit our family (needless to say, our methods shift and adapt as we learn more about each of our four children's personalities, strengths and quirks).

As I progress through the educational journey with my children,

I am becoming more aware of just how much groundwork came naturally to me *because* I was home-educated. We second-generation home educators have had the privilege of watching our parents muddle through a pioneering stage of home education. I've watched and learnt from my parents' triumphs and mistakes. This has been mostly intuitive but, a decade into home educating my own children, I'm now beginning to recognise how deeply I've been influenced by their trailblazing.

This is particularly the case when it comes to the rhythms of my days and the little traditions that I didn't even realise that I carried from my parents' home into our young family's life. Sally Clarkson talks often of how reassuring anchors and traditions are. In 'Awaking Wonder', she describes "rhythms of life as anchors in our days, those things that held us fast, that were our moorings to keep us from drifting in the winds of life" (2020, p.192). Unconsciously, many of my parents' daily anchors were brought forward into the lives of their grandchildren!

It's why, whenever possible, I automatically instigate 'Quiet Time' after lunch – a time for each of us to recharge, away from each other in (relative) quiet. It shows itself again in the way that I organise our bookshelves to make it easy to find the book that a child needs. The daily tidy-up before dinnertime to keep on top of the chaos of the day (humorously called 'the Daddy Dash' in our home and 'EHAP' – 'Everything Has A Place').

No-one had to tell me the warning signs that indicate I need to adapt or change the material a child is learning from – tears (from parent or child) are a particular warning sign! I had an innate habit of buying schoolbooks and material for the children's birthdays (this has recently been banned by my unamused children because they cottoned on to what I was doing).

Not everything that worked for my parents fits my own style or the spread of characters that are my children. I'm a very different personality from my introverted mother and our home education choices naturally reflect that. Each family is unique and it would be crazy to shoehorn my children into the same style that worked for my parents. Instinctively, I positively adapt and tweak educational approaches, influenced by the choices my parents had to struggle through when I was growing up. It's been an unconscious gleaning of ideas.

With all this in mind, I guess you could legitimately say that I and other second-generation home educators have had a head-start at this gig.

**Is there a difference?**

When asked about the value of home education, many home-educated adults list the same character traits that their background has shaped in them. Regardless of the educational choices we make for the next generation, these are generally all perceived advantages that set us apart from many traditionally schooled peers.

Having had an 'outside-of-the-box' upbringing, we are often comfortable with fostering an independence of mind even when it means we stand out from the crowd. We have learnt that it is alright, and sometimes a great strength, to be 'different' when we swim against the flow. As young people, we learnt early the importance of self-discipline and responsibility. We value education highly and many of us have an insatiable curiosity about life.

But is there a difference to the approach of second-generation home educators like myself from our friends who are brand new to this? Have we benefitted from standing on the shoulders of home education pioneers? If so, how?

*Culture*

I suppose that an obvious difference between the generations of home educators is the inborn familiarity we have. Unsurprisingly, the second generation are immersed in the lingo and values of the home education subculture. It's already natural to us.

There were far fewer home educators in the UK when my parents started this journey. There was also no internet! So I guess it is not a surprise that my parents knew few named educational philosophies.

But, when Andy and I were new parents researching what shape we wanted education to take in our home, lots of the labels for home education approaches seemed familiar to me as we dug deeper into the methods and philosophies behind them. Unknowingly, I had seen many of these systems in action.

Unit studies, Classical education, Charlotte Mason, unschooling and others (see also Appendix A) – with all the varying overlaps and combinations used by individual families. The second generation already know which of these educational tools will either fit us like a comfortable old jumper or feel like a straitjacket; we have a head-start when picking our methods.

We've watched our parents push on doors to find and ask for deals and activities on offer to schools so that we could also partake. Utilising museums, art galleries, libraries and other facilities is an obvious action to us because the chances are high that our parents learnt to do this for us. More is indeed caught than taught!

Second-generation home educators brought up in Christian homes are well acquainted with the benefits of educating outside government schools. Depending on how articulate our parents were, or how much we, as young people, were actually listening to their reasoning, we already have foundational reasons for the 'why' of Christian home education. Regardless of how perfectly, or imperfectly, our parents lived it out in front of us, we can see the immense value of education as a form of discipleship.

> *"You shall teach them diligently to your children [impressing God's precepts on their minds and penetrating their hearts with His truths] and shall speak of them when you sit in your house and when you walk on the road and when you lie down and when you get up."*
> (Deuteronomy 6:7, Amplified Version)

Carrying home education on to the next generation is the most ideal way for Andy and me to live out this passage in Deuteronomy. How, we ask ourselves, could we do this fully if we chose not to home-educate? As I delve deeper into apologetics as an adult, I am able to better articulate biblical reasons for the importance of nurturing our children in the Lord at home in their early years. Yet the basic structural idea of Christian education was already inbuilt; having been established as a foundation in my life by my parents as they sought to follow the Lord down this educational path.

*Comprehension*

First-generation home-educating adults often know quite naturally what kind of instructional atmosphere they want to nurture in the home environment. This is frequently a subjective understanding based on their own school experience, be it positive or negative. That same instinct holds exactly true for me and my peers! Things that our parents put in place at home which we enjoyed or felt comforted by, we tend to replicate. Maybe these include certain routines to structure our days or educational philosophies to shape our methods. Activities or opportunities that we wish we had experienced but didn't for whatever reason, we seek to provide our own children. Scout groups, ballet or organised sports, perhaps.

Likewise, if we don't want to replicate our parents' teaching approaches, we have the confidence to change to a different method. This could mean changing structure to more formal schooling with set timetables, for example, or, at the other end of the spectrum, unschooling. Maybe our childhood was packed to the brim with activities and we see more downtime as a better option instead. Often, we find the middle ground in a diverse educational spectrum.

I believe that my peers and I have subtle yet distinctive insights into home education. It's not exactly the same for each of us because individual families have different educational journeys. Yet, whether for part of our education or for the whole, our experiences place us in the unique advantage of having actually tasted what it's like to receive this form of education.

*Confidence*

Regardless of how you measure success, home-educated young people can achieve just as much as those in school. From academic performance to relationships. From a humble walk with Christ to positive personal abilities. I feel confident that I'm not holding my children back in any way by choosing an unconventional upbringing. This confidence comes in part because I know that an atypical childhood benefitted me.

This does not mean that we second-generation home educators have all the answers. I still struggle with the same choices and difficulties that new home educators have. However, I know that, if carried out in a loving home which encourages curiosity and wonder, home education works. This holds true regardless of your chosen learning structure and methods. I know this strongly because I saw it work in my life.

The first child in any sibling group is always going to be a guinea pig for the parents. Home-educated children are no different and it is common to see parents become more relaxed in their educational journey as time passes. We find our feet, grow in confidence and fine-tune our ideas as we walk this road. This is just as true for me as I home-educate my children as it is for a parent totally new to this concept of educating.

Over time circumstances change, children develop, technology advances. Tweaks and adjustments are imperative to enable education to continually bring out the best in each child. Several of my younger siblings were still being educated at home when Andy and I started with our children and, through watching my parents over the years, I learnt that flexibility is hugely beneficial. Again, having been on the receiving end of positive changes, I feel secure doing this with my own children.

Home-educating parents simply can't provide for our children every opportunity that we'd like. We can fret about it and strive to spread a broad feast of knowledge and understanding in front of our children, but still we will leave topics unfinished and concepts unmastered. I have to admit that, in the first few years of being a parent and like most home educators, I worried about leaving gaps in my children's education. On reflection, I needn't have fretted.

In her excellent article 'Taking a Bird's Eye View' (2014), Sarah

Mackenzie reminds us that "gaps are gifts"[1]. Second-generation home educators can rest in their own experience of this reality: perceived gaps in education have not actually held us back, but rather fuelled greater interest in, and added enthusiasm for, filling those spaces later on.

A particular difference which stands out between first and second-generation home educators is how we perceive the long-term perspective. If you've had the privilege of receiving home education, you know that this route really does 'work'. Although the experimental factor is, of course, still at play in our homes, we know through experience – which those new to home education can know only in theory – that home educating is a valid, life-broadening, wonderful way to educate. This experiential understanding gives us an underlying confidence into which we dig deep on those (many) harder days.

**Why don't they continue?**

You are likely aware of many of the reasons that hold people back from taking the plunge into home education in the first place: lack of confidence, worries about socialisation, negativity from family and friends, financial restraints, etc. But in addition to this, not all home-educated young people continue on to do the same for their own children. If it really was such a benefit, why is this the case?

We are a few decades into the British home education movement, and we have to admit that it has not been a success for some students and families. This understanding should be held in context, however, lest we throw the baby out with the bathwater. A school education is far more often detrimental, for many more people, by comparison!

With a few exceptions aside, I do not think a first-generation rejection of home education is a sign that educating at home was a failure. Every family is unique and there are so many conflicting voices yelling to be heard, that it can be hard for some home-educated adults starting families to discern what is right for them.

---

[1] https://readaloudrevival.com/taking-birds-eye-view/

But what are some of the more distinct reasons why many home-educated adults choose not to continue? Generalisations can be inaccurate for individuals; however, the most common reasons that I come across seem to be centred on financial restraints and on wanting to give their children a different upbringing from their own.

*Financial restraints*

The majority of home-educating families have two parents and, normatively, the mother will be based at home full-time to educate, and the family lives off the father's single income. Obviously, there is a financial cost to having a parent stay at home to educate children. For families in some parts of the UK, this loss of income is prohibitive.

Andy and I personally consider home education to be so vital to our role as parents that we would rather move to a more affordable area than have both of us employed full-time. I am keenly aware that this is not always an option for many families.

For the majority of single-income families, home education means having to minimise as many financial outgoings as possible. Sacrificing more costly lifestyle options with holiday, housing and transport choices become the only way to make home education possible. Some young adults either don't want to, or simply can't, raise a family on the equivalent of one income.

*Conflict of worldview*

Home education is still an unorthodox educational pathway. It has the capacity to shape the experience of a young person so profoundly that its impact can never be ignored. A differing worldview from their parents affects young adults' understanding of education and can lead to a rejection of that path for their own children.

As children become young adults and grow in independence, they become self-aware and more mindful of other methods of education. Depending on the way they were home-educated, they may feel that they missed out on certain opportunities that they perceive – rightly or wrongly – that they would have accessed through school. Regardless of how accurate or inaccurate their perceptions may be, some see the educational values and choices which their parents made as too extreme or narrow. As a result, they seek the greener grass on the other side of the fence to balance their upbringing.

Sometimes, a failure to feel benefit from home education is due to an unbalanced family structure in which there are relational problems within the home at a very basic level, negatively influencing the home environment.

Just like adults educated in the school system who choose to educate their children at home, if young people feel home education failed them then, of course, they are going to feel less inclined to follow that path with their own children.

*A lack of partner support*

For me, and many other home-educated adults like me, the decision to home-educate was among the early topics of discussion with my future spouse. Educating as much as possible in the home environment doesn't simply dovetail with my understanding of Christian parenting; I believe it has become a vital tool to inoculate our children against increasingly anti-Christian aspects of our secular culture. For me personally, resistance to this point of view would have been a relationship-breaker early on.

However, not everyone feels the same, or holds this concept as strongly. Those who do not share equal resolve with their spouse or who perceive home education as a complementary add-on to parenting will likely give their children a school education. They know home educating equals much parental hard work and they may not have the support or resolve to carry it through.

**Conclusion**

My parents and their peers were trailblazers in the 1980s. They were brave; some would say foolhardy. But so also is every first-generation parent taking the plunge into home education. Take it from me: it truly is worth the sacrifices you are making for your children.

Even though educational variations set me apart from my schooled friends, I am so grateful that my parents gave me an individualised upbringing. It is a huge influence on why Andy and I chose to continue this route for our own children. Our approach looks different to my childhood experience because it is shaped by both our and our children's personalities, but it is home education, nonetheless.

Aside from the multiple challenges of learning to parent for the first time (another topic in itself), I still struggle with finding the 'best fit' material for my children. I question the educational decisions we've made on their behalf. Juggle multiple children and their individual educational needs. Wonder what to do about exams and qualifications. Fight presumptions about socialisation and my concerns about finding them local, close friends. Decision fatigue has exhausted my brain on more days than I care to remember. I have to constantly rediscover the Lord's grace, on my knees, at the foot of the Cross. On almost every level, this is all new to me too.

So, are second-generation home educators standing on the shoulders of giants? I believe that we are. The benefit is subtle but present, often hidden in the day-to-day chaos of the dirty dishes, conflict resolution and the unfinished workbooks that threaten to engulf our days.

Because despite all this, we – the growing ranks of second-generation home educators – have an inner confidence in our 'lived experience' that home education *works*. This is not just simply an ideal to us. We were home-educated and we survived that educational experiment with our parents. In fact, looking back now as parents ourselves, we realise that it helped us thrive as individuals. After all the societal concerns of socialisation, we're content in the knowledge that we're actually no more unusual than the next person.

The second generation of home educators in Britain is growing. We know in our bones, more than the trailblazing first generation ever can, that home education will not just benefit our children but will enhance their lives. That gives us confidence to carry on doing what our parents started.

PART 3

# PART 3: SURVIVAL MODE: TIPS AND TRICKS TO SEE IT THROUGH

## CHAPTER NINE

# MAKING IT WORK: OVERCOMING CHALLENGES, COMPLICATIONS AND CURVEBALLS

# PART 1 – WHEN EVERYTHING IS STACKED AGAINST YOU

*Kirsteen McLeod*

The first time we attended our local home education group, I felt somewhat overwhelmed. Every other family seemed very 'normal'. Dual-parent families with hands-on dads, disposable income and big family cars. Their children were well turned out with good manners, and they generally did what they were told. They ate healthy and nutritious home-cooked meals and they were clearly receiving a rich education, including music, art, languages, science and so much more. I went home and cried.

We were not a 'normal' family. I was a lone parent without an income, living on benefits, with a clapped-out old banger that stopped more than it started. Two of my three children were showing signs that they might have autism and might require considerably more care and support than the average child. They were high energy and selectively hard of hearing; they mostly ate chicken nuggets and definitely never said 'How high?' whenever I said 'Jump'. How would we ever fit in, and how could we possibly walk along the same road as other families who were supposedly taking the same journey and yet whose lives looked so very different to ours?

Less than a year earlier, my husband had walked out the door and I was fairly certain that we might never see him again. At the time my children were 4, 2 and 10 months old – a bright little girl and two inquisitive baby boys. I didn't have a job. I was a stay-at-home mum by choice. I had given up my career and intentionally chosen to be at home to raise my babies. And to be honest, having had three babies in three years, the cost of childcare would have made it not worth working anyway. The day after my husband left, I found out our bank account had been emptied – maxed up to a new and very high overdraft limit he had applied for without my knowledge or consent, and he'd cleared out the lot. He'd also cleared out our savings. Every penny, gone. In that moment I knew we couldn't rely on him for any financial contribution. I was quite literally penniless, with three babies I couldn't even buy nappies for, let alone a mortgage I definitely couldn't afford to pay.

All I had was three children I loved more than anything in the world, and a conviction to stay at home with them and home-educate them. For two years I had been seeking God about it, and I believed with all my heart that He was actually calling me to home-educate my children. That conviction had started as a tiny seed two years previously, which over time had been cultivated until it had blossomed into a dream. The dream was to be fully involved in my children's upbringing and education for as long as they needed me to be. It was more than a dream, actually, as it was the very rhythm and beat of my heart, and it suddenly seemed impossible now.

## CHAPTER NINE

**A journey of faith**

The decision had been made months before. I had started planning, purchasing and preparing. Our home education journey would begin shortly after my daughter's 4th birthday. And yet here we were, the week of her 4th birthday, and my husband was gone. I was on my own, with no job, no money and three little ones. I felt completely empty-handed and didn't see how we could begin that journey now. But what I did have was just a little bit of faith.

As a Christian it's easy for me to talk about faith. Everything I am and everything I do hinges upon it. But regardless of whether someone is a person of faith or no faith, home education requires faith. It is a faith journey. What I mean by that is that it takes a lot of faith to home-educate. Faith that this thing you believe in does actually work, and that the end result will be worth all the hard work and sacrifice. Faith that you are not completely ruining your child's life and education, and that they will come out the other side a fully functioning human, despite any seeming blips along the way. Every home educator needs to have faith: faith in both the journey upon which they are embarking and the final destination for which they are heading – or else we simply wouldn't be able to do it. That's why I call it a faith journey.

However, as a Christian I also had another kind of faith: faith that my God would somehow make a way for us, and would provide us with what we needed to make it work, even with everything in our circumstances stacked against us, and with the vast majority of our friends and family firmly opposed to our decision to home-educate. I carried an assurance in my heart that God would help us to figure it all out and would help to make a way for us. My reason for this assurance? Less than a week after becoming a lone parent I had a wobble and decided I had no choice but to lay the dream down. God spoke to me very clearly and reminded me that He knows and sees everything. He knew this was going to happen, and He had already stirred the dream in my heart and allowed it to be birthed. He told me to go ahead and take this journey and promised He would make a way for us and provide us with everything we would need along the way.

Over the days and weeks that followed, I managed to apply for Income Support and some other benefits, and these became our primary income while we navigated through the rest of the baby and toddler years. It didn't cover everything, but it put food on the table and covered most of the bills. As predicted, my husband completely abandoned us financially and wouldn't contribute to anything, not even for the children. He even tried to sell our home, which we jointly owned, without telling me. He put it on the market and the first I knew about it was when the estate agent arrived and put a 'For Sale' sign up. My husband wanted us out so he could sell the house and seemed quite happy to make us homeless in the process. There was no equity in the house, so he wasn't going to benefit from selling it. He wasn't contributing to any costs concerning the house, so it wasn't costing him anything. From his point of view, it made no financial difference whether it was sold or not, but he wanted it sold anyway and didn't seem to care what happened to his children.

Every time we hit an obstacle, and a seemingly massive brick wall in front of us, I would pray, "Lord, You said You would make a way for us, even where there is no way. Right now there is no way here, so I need You to make one." And He did. We saw the Lord work in many wonderful and miraculous ways. My husband eventually stopped fighting me on the house and gave up any rights he had to it. My solicitor managed to get it fully signed over to me. We are still there now, all these years later, and never once defaulted on a mortgage payment. For those first couple of years in particular, most months I didn't have the money for the mortgage. But the Lord always made up for the shortfall, and money always arrived on time. He provided for any lack we had. He provided envelopes of cash through the door, new cars whenever we needed them, new appliances whenever old ones died, clothes and toys for the children, holidays when we needed one, money to buy educational supplies, money at birthdays and Christmas to buy the children gifts, and money for oil to fuel our central heating system. He provided everything we needed, time and time again. And then as the children started to get bigger, He provided work for me to do that I could fit around my family's needs.

**A steep and rocky climb**

Having worked through those early days of fighting to keep our home and trying to figure out our finances, and with our home education journey well underway, I had started to realise that both my boys were not hitting their developmental milestones in the standard way, and I was seeing things that concerned me. I started to realise that they might have autism. Both were diagnosed, and in the years since we have added a collective array of other comorbid issues, including anxiety, processing delay, learning challenges and query ADHD and OCD (still not fully conclusive either way). So, in addition to being a lone parent I was now also a carer and an advocate for my boys, and had to spend a massive amount of time figuring out how their autism affected them, and what tools they needed me to help them find and use in order to live their best lives and fulfil their potential. It was another very steep learning curve after what had already felt like a steep and rocky climb.

But God has always been faithful. Not once has He let us down or abandoned us. He has led me through every challenge and directed me many times to take a particular course of action. He has also given me dozens of creative ideas to help the boys get unstuck when they have been overwhelmed with life. He is good, and compassionate, and gracious, and merciful. That is who He is!

We are now 16 years on from 'that day' that changed our life completely. My children haven't seen their dad in all those years. We have managed to juggle work and home education for multiple years. We managed to get some support for my boys from a local charity, and we've managed to navigate them through an education that has been appropriate for their needs. Both of them are thriving and becoming increasingly independent as each year goes past, and they have recently started part-time at a local college with a view to attending full-time within the next couple of years. My daughter has now 'graduated' from home education with a solid set of qualifications and is taking a year out to help support her brothers in getting to college when I'm working, while also working part-time herself. All three of them are actively involved in local church and in their community in different ways. They are musical, gifted, artistic, compassionate human beings. We did it! We have successfully home educated for 16 years (and counting), because God did it for us. He made a way for us.

## Uniting faith with determination

I get asked a lot, "How exactly did you make it all work? I've only got one child and a husband and I'm not sure I can do this. But you have done it alone, in very challenging circumstances. How?" This is where I could rattle off all the practicalities of the 'how'. I could talk about things like being a team and all sharing the chores. I could talk about prioritising time and energy for the most important things. I could talk about how some nights of the week I just fire shop-bought pizza or frozen chicken nuggets into the oven because that saves some time on a busy evening, or how I try to prioritise relationships in the house over very boring things like housework (I do clean my house sometimes, it's just not always our biggest priority). I could talk about all the luxuries we gave up and all the things we sacrificed, and how we focused our spending so that we could afford to home-educate.

In terms of working, after our initial spell on Income Support, I set up in business as a registered childminder and ran a very successful childcare setting from our home. When some unexpected health problems a few years later made chasing small people too challenging, I set up a small arts and crafts business instead, taking commissions for personalised gifts and artwork and travelling around craft fairs to sell my wares. In both cases, I home-educated around my work, but my work was an education in itself in many ways, and I always found ways to involve my children in the running of my businesses. In both cases I was based at home and didn't need to worry about childcare. I made sure I stayed at home with my children until my eldest was over the age of 16 and able to help look after her siblings without feeling overwhelmed, at which point I could start considering other options. In 2019 I took my first job out of the house. Ironically, after a few short months the pandemic hit, and I've ended up working from home again. By that point all my children were of an age where they could study with minimal input from me, so it felt like the right time to try something different.

But I guess the biggest 'how' for me, along with an awful lot of faith and trust, was sheer determination. I've been told I'm a little stubborn at times. I can accept that. But I don't think stubbornness is always a bad thing. There is a fine line between stubbornness and determination, when used for something good. When most of my family and friends lined up to tell me that I couldn't possibly home-educate as a lone parent, my somewhat stubborn and internal response was, 'You just watch me!' And that stubbornness kickstarted a major dose of determination. I was just so determined that no matter what, I would do whatever I needed to do, whatever it took, because these were my babies. I loved them more than words could describe, and I would have moved heaven and earth for them. I was determined to do absolutely everything in my power to stay at home with them, however creative I needed to be, for as long as possible – however little sleep I got – to be able to nurture them and educate them, and nothing was going to stand in the way of that. That sheer determination, in hand with believing that my God would take care of all the bits that were completely outside my power, is what has kept me going for 16 years.

The thing about that union of faith and determination (or stubbornness!) is that we don't need to deny our limitations while trusting that God will provide. I had many limitations along the way. I still do. There were things I found hard, times I was overwhelmed, times I was plain exhausted, times my health was poor, times I fell out with God, and plenty of times when financially I just couldn't meet my family's needs. But God always shows Himself strongest when we are at our weakest, and He has more than compensated for my weaknesses and failings as we have walked this journey. It has been a journey of great grace and deep dependence on Him – utterly nail-biting, edge-of-my-seat, stubborn, determined, faith-filled yet imperfect, dependence on God.

No family is perfect, and nobody has the perfect set of circumstances to home-educate. We all have hurdles to overcome at some point and curve balls to either dodge, or catch and hold on to for a while – they just look different for each of us. Maybe you are reading this and you have already discounted yourself as a home educator, purely because of your own unique circumstances. What I tell people is that if my family can do it, anyone can. If you have a conviction that home education is the right thing for your child, and you have even a small amount of faith that it could work, and enough determination and creativity to do whatever you need in order to make it all hang together, you can absolutely home-educate. On the good days and the bad days, and on the 'it's all falling apart and I don't think I can go on' days (there will be at least a few of those), just trust, believe, dare to dream, and ask God to make a way for you.

# PART 2 – A WORKING MUM AND A HOME-EDUCATING DAD

*Matthew Harris*

This chapter is about how people have made home education work for their family's unique circumstances. If you're anything like me, you will have probably jumped into this chapter wanting to know the 'how tos' and now you'll be scanning the pages for practical advice that you can use straight away. In order to help my kindred spirits, my 'advice' (if one can call it that), can be summarised under the following headings:

- Communicate well
- Budget
- Agree on roles and play to your strengths
- Communicate again
- Get involved
- Take a break
- Find a community
- Make sure you keep communicating

There you have it: that pretty much summarises what I have to offer. What follows simply puts some 'flesh on the bones' of the list above.

**Our story**

My wife and I are not 'normal'. Amongst our peers and our family members we are the outliers, the ones that have chosen a slightly different 'lifestyle path' to everyone else. For a start, we are home-educating, but you know that already. Nicola is, at the time of writing, a curate in the Church of England. This too is not the norm. And even within our home education community we are unusual as Nicola is the one that is out at work, earning a crust, whilst I, Matt, am one of a rare breed of home-educating dads.

We started home-educating when Nicola started her training at Trinity College in Bristol. We moved there from Surrey, where I was a youth worker at a church and Nicola was a part-time self-employed occupational therapist. Up until our move to Bristol, our two daughters had been in mainstream school (both in the same, really good, nurturing primary school) but we had started to consider home education as a viable option ever since our good friends had started home educating and had seen their children thrive. We were possibly only going to be in Bristol for a couple of years whilst Nicola studied, so to minimise the disruption to our daughters' lives we thought we would join up with our friends and home-educate our children together. We are now into our fourth year of this home education journey and what follows is a picture of how we have made it work as a family where the dad is at home and the mum is out at work.

**How we make it work: tips and principles**

The first thing is to have a shared idea of what home education is, a common vision, as it were. More crucially, it's about working out together what you think is important for your children: what sort of people do you want them to be? What are the values that you want to expose them to and instil in them? Learning facts and how to do things is actually secondary (in my opinion) and, as a couple, you will disagree on what's vital in their formal education (times tables are one of those issues in our household), but you can agree that you want your children to be (or at least have the opportunity to be) creative, kind, confident, curious, caring ... Keeping these end goals in view puts everything else in perspective. And that includes learning times tables.

Ever since we have started home educating, we've been aware that it costs. It costs money. It costs time. It costs your original hair colour. But I suppose you can say that about parenting in general (and we can testify that it's also worth every penny, second, grey hair and wrinkle)!

It's a really good idea to work out a budget and to make the home education fit the budget rather than the other way around. Yes, your children may miss out on a few opportunities, but putting financial pressure on your family for the sake of an extra activity or group is just not worth it. As I mentioned, when we started Nicola was studying, so our income was the lowest we'd had for a while. We went from being an almost double-income family to being on a single student bursary. Fortunately, Nicola is a brilliant budgeter and we have family who have been very kind and generous and have supported us through the last few years. It would have been very difficult without them. We are very privileged and recognise that not everyone can afford to live on a single income.

What follows on from this is that we try to play to our strengths. I'm a natural educator. I love learning and so it follows that I would be the one who did the home education. Our circumstances also determined who was at work and who was at home, although we ultimately did have a choice. I don't find planning or budgeting easy, but Nicola is fabulous at both, so leads the way with those things. She is very organised – I am not – so it follows that she helps out with that side of our home education. For example, recently, Nicola has been producing monthly plans for our girls so that they know what is coming up.

There is a tension with just playing to your strengths, however, as there is great opportunity to be had in children seeing how their parents learn how to do things that aren't in their 'sweet spot'. Additionally, it can be very beneficial for the non-home-educating parent to get involved when and where they can. Nicola's present work schedule means that she can take the girls to different groups. This keeps their relationship going, she sees what they are up to (even home-educated children can be very minimal in their response to the question, "How was your day today?"!) and it gives me a bit of a break!

This segues beautifully into the next point. We try to make sure that we each have time to rest and have time to ourselves. Being the parent at home can be mentally, emotionally and even physically demanding. For a start, you're always in your workplace (I can imagine generations of women looking at me right now and thinking, "Only now you're realising this?!") and there is always something that could be done. But burnout is real. And just as it is important that the 'breadwinner' is able to rest when at home, it's crucial that the home-based parent gets a break too. We've found that having a 'sabbath' (a day of rest each week) as a family has been very valuable. Taking time to reconnect with each other has been so good. Establishing good family rhythms and traditions can help keep the family moving in the same direction (and in the same room for a few minutes, too).

With all of the above, we've found it so helpful, useful and life-giving to be a part of a wider home education community. It's good for us (we know that we're not on our own) and it's brilliant for our children. Our girls have loved meeting up regularly with a group of people with whom they work on learning projects or simply hang out and have fun. As well as the social aspect of these groups, being a part of a home education community means that you can share resources and talents and speak into the wider world of home education. We have run so many sessions and enjoyed learning opportunities in this community that would have been incredibly difficult to create just as a singular family unit. Also, there is bound to be someone in your network that is very good at resourcing home educators. We have a good friend who is excellent at finding deals (or asking for them) and opportunities for learning in our area.

## CHAPTER NINE

So that's a snapshot of how we've made it work as a family, with me as a home-educating dad to our two daughters and Nicola as the one working full-time outside of the home, but still being involved with her daughters' development and education. I hope it is of use.

# PART 3 - THE STRUGGLE TO JUGGLE

*Afia Bayayi*

My name is Afia and I'm a home-educating mum of three. At the point of writing, my children are aged 8, 6 and 4. They've always been home-educated. Our home education schedule is quite packed with activities and classes. I'm a mum who knows how to keep her children busy!

As well as being solely responsible for their education, I run a business in weddings and events. Being self-employed is all-consuming. It can be very difficult to switch off. Running the business comes with so many responsibilities and daily things to do (what's more, the challenging thing about working with brides-to-be is that they often expect their wedding to be at the centre of your universe!). At this stage of my entrepreneurial journey, I still wear the many hats of bookkeeping, dealing with enquiries, sales, client liaison, invoices and payments, marketing, research, staffing, social media, making purchases and being the creative driving everything.

If that wasn't enough, my husband is the pastor of our church. It goes without saying that to be in the ministry is a life of sacrifice and service. The role is a huge demand on my husband's time and a major responsibility for which he needs my support – and he does it all whilst working part-time.

So how do I do it? This is a question I am often asked, because all the above is in addition to making time for my personal relationship with God, self-care, general adult duties and fulfilling my roles as a daughter, sister and friend, as well as being intentional with family time.

The honest answer is that it is often a struggle to juggle everything. It can get extremely overwhelming. As I write this, I'm recovering from Covid-19. It was a perfect storm because I was already quite run down from back-to-back weddings during a wedding season like no other, caused by a backlog of 2020 weddings in combination with 2021 bookings. So, when I caught Covid, I completely crashed. My husband was thrilled for me; he often says to me, "If you do not find rest, rest will find you!" To be sincere, the driven workaholic in me finds it difficult to rest without feeling guilty or somewhat irresponsible for not being 'productive with my time'. However, during the forced period of rest, I was able to put together my contribution to this book, tune into the messages my body has been sending me, think deeply and practise stillness. God indeed knew the importance of rest, which is why He dedicated a day of the week to it. Every single week. So, one thing I am going to do when I review my timetable for the next school term is implement periods of rest for myself. In life, if we don't make time for something, it seldom happens.

That's right, I have a timetable. It's the secret sauce to the Bayayi household. I try to run a home that is well organised and generally kept tidy and clean. I have the conviction that our God is a God of order and not chaos or confusion, and that shapes how I structure the day and manage my time, as well as how I keep our home. Our children find safety in this type of environment and they find security in structure and routine. The timetable I have drawn up has copies around the house to keep me accountable to the children. It is also a great point of reference for everyone, especially my husband, who is the most forgetful person I know.

There is time allocated for me to spend time in prayer and devotion and to shower undisturbed, early in the morning, before the children wake up. When I start the day right, this helps everybody else. As the saying goes, the woman is often the thermostat of the home! Morning time is an important part of the day for us and sets the tone and mood of the rest of the day. I enjoy the opportunity to engage in conversation with my children about deep and important topics that help to connect us as a family. I allocate time for meal prep and factor in when I need to get ready to leave the house for certain classes and activities. Leaving at the designated time reduces the likelihood of running late, which means I will be less irritable with the children. There is time allocated for each lesson by subject, as well as time for them to read to me and to go outside and get fresh air. We have a bedtime for the children and a routine to accompany this, which follow a dinnertime that is shared at the table as a family.

In putting our timetable together, I sat down and considered everything that was important for us to achieve on a weekly basis. Whatever was of enough value to make regular time for made it to the family timetable. As a point of reference, it has been fantastic for helping us to be good stewards of our time. To complement this, I set alarms on my phone to remind me of where we are supposed to be and when. The children are now experienced in yelling out, "Mum, it says it's time to leave now; we've got to go!"

As regimented as all this may sound, I do allow for flexibility with it as I appreciate that 'life' happens. So, though it provides a fantastic framework to guide each day, it is not fixed or immovable. I tweak and amend our timetable often, upon reflection on what does or does not work, for each of us. There have been days when I've ditched the timetable, got the children to put their wellington boots on and gone for walks in the rain with them. There have also been busy periods when I've decided to put a pause on the timetable just to accommodate the ebbs and flows of life.

Lastly, what has helped greatly is keeping a 'Things to Do' book. I have a page-a-day diary which I use to document my list of things to do for each day. At the beginning of each week, I pen down what I can for the week ahead, and break each day into segments including: 'Who I need to call/message', 'Emails that need to be sent', Payments that need to be made', 'Outstanding housework' and 'Life admin'.

Keeping a 'Things to Do' book is a discipline I have maintained since I was in 6th Form, and it has honestly revolutionised my life. I have so many things to remember/stay on top of at any given time and doing this really helps. I can't begin to describe to you the overwhelming feeling of satisfaction I get from crossing off an item on that list. It's a strategy I highly recommend for home-educating parents who also work in some capacity.

I'm one of the busiest people I know. Structure, routine and orderliness have saved me from having complete meltdowns. I just need to get the balance right with enough time for rest and relaxation and, by God's grace, I believe I'll be stepping into the direction of the no-struggle juggle a lot more.

CHAPTER TEN

# SELF-CARE MATTERS: TEN WAYS TO LOOK AFTER YOURSELF AND AVOID BURNOUT

*Catherine Shelton*

I wave my husband and children goodbye and watch our family car turn down the driveway. Picking up my bag, I make my way to the reception and check in. The atmosphere at this lovely Christian retreat centre is just how I remember it. A friendly face directs me up the stairs where the key to my room for the next two nights is waiting in the lock. As I close the door behind me, I sigh with contentment. I open the window and gaze out briefly onto the flower-bordered, freshly mown lawn below. A set of complimentary teas and coffees sits on a tray next to my bed, and I notice a thoughtful welcome card lying on the pillow.

I consider my plans for the day: a cup of tea with a good book; a gentle stroll down to the beach; a peaceful nap where I won't be disturbed. And, of course, a lovely evening meal where someone else will be cooking and washing up. My neck and shoulders begin to relax as the stress of the past six rather difficult months starts to lift. I know that two days from now I'll be ready to return home to my family – a much more relaxed, energised, revitalised and joyful version of myself.

## What is self-care, and isn't it selfish?

All parents face busy, hectic and stressful times, and home-educating parents are no different. Thankfully, we have avoided having to deal with endless forms and communication with the school, or the early morning scramble to get children dressed, fed and out of the house on time with their packed lunch and PE kit. And don't even get me started on piecing together last-minute costumes for the latest project on the Romans or World Book Day!

But home education isn't always plain sailing either. There are days when one or more of us is sick, or a child just doesn't want to do their maths or reading that day. The children are squabbling over the felt tip pens, we might have been up all night with a little one, and we still have to put a picnic together for the local home education meet-up.

Perhaps one of the most challenging aspects of home education is that, well, our children are always at home! We can try to tidy up the living room and wipe down the kitchen counters, but chances are there will be a new fort up or a messy cookery project underway within five minutes. Any shopping that we need to do, whether it's the weekly food shop or hunting for this year's Christmas gifts, probably has to be done with some or all of the children in tow, which doesn't make it any more relaxing.

Don't get me wrong, home education is amazing. We're just coming to the end of our eleventh year, with four children, and we wouldn't change it for the world. But that doesn't mean that I'm not ... well ... rather tired!

Enter self-care.

"But I don't deserve any time to myself."
"I need to meet everyone else's needs first."
"A good parent shouldn't need time off."
"I'd just feel guilty if I went off to the café by myself."

Have you ever thought any of the above? Probably. Because you wouldn't have even considered home education if you weren't already a wonderful, committed, caring parent who wants the very best for their children. It goes without saying, home education is not the easy option!

Sacrificing your time and even your career for your children's education is a noble thing. But if you get burned out while doing it, then you're not really helping anyone in the long run.

And I hate to say this, but at the end of the day, the children won't remember so much about the periodic table and the reign of Henry VIII as they will the atmosphere that surrounded their experience of being educated at home. Will they remember times of fun, laughter, adventures and new experiences, or will they remember the fact that you were always complaining about being stressed and tired? It's no use being at your children's beck and call 24/7 if they're constantly walking around on eggshells so as not to awaken the monster that is 'Shouty Mummy' (don't ask me how I know).

**Ten essential elements of taking care of yourself**

You've probably heard of the analogy of the oxygen mask: how, just like we're told in the pre-flight safety demonstration to fix our own oxygen masks first before we help our children with theirs, we need to make sure that our own needs are being met before we can give our best to those around us. Or perhaps you've heard the line, 'You can't pour out of an empty cup'.

The theory is the same. If we persistently neglect our own basic needs, then our families will suffer. Notice I said 'persistently'. Of course, there are times when we're in the middle of a crisis and we just have to batten down the hatches and do the best with what we have. But once the storm is over and the sun comes out again, that's the time to continue being intentional about how we're caring for ourselves, day in, day out. We're going to survive future storms much better if we have this in place first.

As a health coach, I've had the opportunity to research this topic and observe the lives of my own clients, and what I've noticed is that we all have basic areas of self-care that need working on simultaneously. Health and wellness are holistic endeavours. It's no good focussing on one area to the detriment of others. Self-care is not just about taking a break. Or booking yourself in for a spa day. It's so much more than that, and what one person needs to show up as their best self may look very different to what another person needs.

What follows are ten elements of self-care that all work together to help you live up to your fullest potential as a home-educating parent and help you flourish in this challenging but extremely rewarding walk of life. They are in no particular order, but pay attention to each one and give yourself a score out of ten on how you think you're doing in that area.

*1) Sleep*

Did I just hear you laugh sarcastically? If your children are still very small, you might not remember the last time you got to sleep through the night. If so, please remember that this is just a season and you will come through it. But, at the end of the day, a good night's sleep is one of the best things we can do for our health and wellbeing on so many levels.

A persistent lack of sleep is strongly correlated with chronic diseases, inflammation, weight gain, dementia and depression. Conversely, consistent good sleep results in better mood and memory function, better performance and greater concentration. When we get the recommended 7-9 hours of sleep a night, we actually get more done, not less. We will be more productive, have more energy and be happier.

When you are home-educating, the temptation can be to let those magical hours after about 8pm drag on too long. The children are finally in bed and at last you have some 'me time'. Having rest and down-time is really important, but faced with a choice of 'just one more episode of the latest BBC drama' or one extra hour of sleep, it's the sleep that will benefit you the most by far.

If you struggle with insomnia, then it's critical that you take steps to address it. Waking up and going to bed at roughly the same time each day, even at the weekends, will help your body regulate its circadian clock. What about the environment you're sleeping in? A small investment in a sleep mask and ear plugs can make a big difference. Be sure to turn off screens at least an hour before you turn off the light, and drastically reduce your caffeine and alcohol intake.

*2) Rest*

Not only do we need a good night's sleep, but we also need times of rest during the day to relax and recharge. And no, I'm not talking about locking yourself in the bathroom for an extra five minutes with your phone while little fingers push paper notes under the door asking when you're coming out!

Rest could be allowing yourself to sit down in the garden with a cup of tea, or on the sofa with a good book. It could be taking your children to the playground and sitting on the bench watching them and the world go by. Or taking a 20-minute power nap while the children are occupied elsewhere. It could be taking time out to close your eyes and do some deep breathing exercises.

Are you aware of your breathing? Most of us spend our days shallow breathing from the top of the chest. But if you watch a baby, you'll notice that it breathes from its belly. Slow, diaphragmatic breathing signals to our bodies that we're safe, and it's one of the best ways we can move ourselves out of the stressful 'fight or flight' state and into the healing 'rest and digest' state. Aim to do four slow, deep breaths at least once a day. Breathe in through your nose for a count of four, hold for a count of seven, and breathe out through your mouth for a count of eight.

Whatever you decide to do for more rest, though, it rarely involves your phone, so put that away out of reach! Scrolling through Instagram, checking the news or updating your status on Facebook is not going to be part of your daily rest time.

*3) Nutrition*

Good nutrition is actually part of self-care. We might think we're being a good parent by putting all our energy into feeding the children and then either picking at their sausages and chips or grabbing that quick, and often unhealthy, snack so that we don't have to cook a whole other meal for ourselves. But just because we can't get our children to eat broccoli no matter how hard we try, doesn't mean that we should avoid it ourselves.

Our bodies need nutrients to function properly. We want to be getting these from whole foods, the way nature intended, especially from a variety of colourful vegetables and fruit. The problem is, much of our diet nowadays is filled with ultra-processed foods that our bodies struggle to digest and that cause inflammation and eventually a whole host of unwelcome conditions and diseases, not to mention weight gain. They're cheap and easy and quick, but they're not serving us in any way.

Does your diet need an overhaul? You might be surprised at how much it affects your mood and your energy levels. And shedding a few extra pounds naturally through eating more whole, plant foods might help you keep up with your children on that bike ride.

In addition, making sure that we're drinking a good amount of water each day and taking essential vitamins is important if we want to function at our best.

### 4) Exercise

Sadly, too many people equate exercise with sweating it out at the gym in order to lose weight. Actually, the impact on weight loss is really minimal compared to the impact from our diet. The 'calories in, calories out' theory was debunked ages ago.

So, does that mean we're off the hook with exercise? Of course not. Exercise has so many other wonderful benefits, especially in terms of heart health, blood pressure regulation, bone and muscle density, and optimal digestion. Exercise also has wonderful benefits on your mood, thanks to those lovely endorphins, and can help alleviate stress and reduce the risk of depression.

The best form of exercise is the kind that you'll actually keep on doing. There's no point starting a gruelling online programme that you know you won't be able to keep up with. Instead, try to find something you enjoy and build from there. Walking, bike riding, running, salsa classes, swimming – whatever works for you. Ideally you want a combination of cardio-based exercise and strength training each week if you can. When my children were young, we all enjoyed some fun workout DVDs together that involved hand-held weights. Later, I found that going for runs along our local seafront was a wonderful stress-reliever for me and helped to get me out of the house. I coupled that with a weekly HIIT session with a personal trainer friend who lived down the road.

*5) Morning routine*

Having some kind of morning routine, even if you wouldn't consider yourself a morning person, is another aspect of self-care. Early mornings are usually the best time to incorporate a few helpful habits, because you can usually be consistent. Your willpower is at its strongest in the morning, and it's easier to be more in control before life happens and the day runs away from you. First thing in the morning, you get to set the tone for the day ahead, and you're not working to someone else's agenda.

Here are some ideas for what to include in your morning routine: reading the Bible, doing a devotional study, spending time in prayer, journalling, reading a personal development book, drinking a glass of water, doing some stretches, taking a walk, listening to worship music, lifting some weights, writing in a gratitude journal, checking your diary and planning the day ahead.

You don't have to get up really early to do this! Depending on your family situation, if you can get up just 15 minutes or so before your children then that will still be beneficial. As you get into the habit, you can then extend that to 30 minutes, or even a bit longer.

I personally notice that if I start my day in this way then the rest of the day goes so much more smoothly, and I feel much more relaxed and in control.

## *6) Alone time*

Everyone needs alone time, but if you're an introvert like me this is also an essential part of your self-care. Introverts recharge their batteries when they're alone, and when you're living in a busy, noisy household (a.k.a. a normal home-educating family), you actually need to be intentional about scheduling this in, otherwise it just won't happen. It's important to remember you're a person in your own right, who needs time just to think, learn, process and grow.

I'm blessed to have a husband who works from home and has flexibility in his work hours. Ever since the children were quite little, we arranged the weekly timetable so that he was able to spend every Wednesday afternoon with the children while I had some 'me time'. I really valued those Wednesdays, and he could see how much it benefitted the whole family to have a more rested, happy Mummy.

Sometimes I would use the time to run a few errands, but I always made sure that at least part of the time was not just 'ticking things off my to-do list'. It might be reading a book in a coffee shop, meeting up with a friend, or taking a walk along the beach. I even ended up taking a few online courses, writing and publishing two novels, and starting up my own health coaching business as a result of my Wednesday afternoons!

I realise not everyone is fortunate to have such flexibility in their family. However, perhaps you can hire a babysitter once a week, or do a swap with another home-educating friend? Or maybe your alone time could happen at the weekend when your partner is around. But whatever you can manage, be sure to schedule it into the diary on a regular basis, and protect that time as being a valuable part of your self-care routine.

## *7) Community*

The opposite of alone time is time in community with others, and we need both. Extroverts especially need time spent with other people, as this is the primary way they recharge their batteries. But the importance of community goes way beyond that.

Human beings flourish best in community with other human

beings. In a fascinating study of the 'Blue Zones' of the world, where people tend to live the longest, the Japanese island of Okinawa came out in the top five. There are various reasons why Okinawa has so many people living long, healthy lives, often to over 100, but one of the reasons is community. Many residents are placed into small groups called Moais from the age of five or so. The Moais give each other support and friendship, and they continue meeting in these groups weekly for up to 90 years!

We might think we get plenty of community just by being home educators. Well, that's great if you're often out and about meeting others or joining in with home education groups and other activities. For some of us, though, we might be more isolated. That was certainly true of us. I tried really hard to find other families I connected with, but we didn't find that many. It's not always easy finding another home-educating family whose values you share, where you get on with the other parent and the children all get on with each other!

Thankfully, there are plenty of places to find community and friendship. Your local church is an obvious example. Or perhaps through a hobby, like a choir, book club or sports team. Sometimes, though, you might be the one needed to reach out and set something up. When we first moved into our town, I was desperate for friends, but I soon realised that everyone else already had their friendship circles sorted. I was going to have to take the initiative. I started up a couple of mums' groups that met in my house once or twice a month. One of those is still going, seven years later, and we've all become great friends!

It's important not to become isolated, so take stock of where you currently find your community and tribe. What can you do to take the initiative if you need to?

*8) Creativity*

Whenever I ask new clients what they do for creativity, they're always a little surprised. But it gets them thinking. Just like we're all built for community, I also believe that we're all made to be creative. It will look different for different people, but part of self-care is making time for hobbies and interests that light you up and allow you to express your creativity.

It might be playing an instrument, painting or drawing. It could be knitting, sewing or crochet. Perhaps, like me, you enjoy writing or blogging. Maybe you love taking photographs, gardening or doing DIY projects. Baking or cake-decorating could be your special talent. One client even came up with the idea of knot-tying as something she'd like to take up!

I believe that creativity is especially important for home-educating parents because so much of our daily work is often 'undone'. We clean, cook and do laundry, but the next day we have to do it all over again. We tidy up one room, only to have the mess return just a few hours later. We cajole our children to do their maths sheet or read the next chapter in the history book, and then have the exact same conversation the next day too.

Having your own, personal creative outlet can be life-giving. You can actually produce something that has beauty and will last. Like a painting, or a quilt, or a collection of blog posts. If baking is your thing, though, you might need to take photographs of your efforts before they're devoured by the hungry hordes!

## 9) Nature – time outside

It has long been known that being out in nature is restorative and beneficial for our health and wellbeing. The Japanese have a lovely term: *Shinrin-yoku*. It means 'forest-bathing'. How often do you go forest-bathing?

It's been shown than the colour green is the most relaxing colour for our eyes. Spending time in nature boosts our happiness and wellbeing and can help to minimise feelings of anxiety and depression, as well as lower blood pressure and improve cognitive function.

Being home educators makes this element of self-care quite easy. In our family, we follow a Charlotte Mason curriculum (see also Appendix A), where nature study is a key part of the children's learning. From an early age, the children all had a nature diary, and we would go out to a local park or wooded area and hunt for interesting things to put in our diaries. We identified plants, pressed flowers, did bark rubbings, collected pine cones, and drew pictures of what we saw using pencils and water colours.

Of course, you don't need to be doing nature study to go outside. We have a 'quiet times' pass to a local country park (another perk of home education – going to usually busy places when everyone else is at school!) where there's a fantastic, wooded play-trail. You could take a picnic to the beach, walk along the river, take a bike ride, or even just spend time in your own garden.

Sometimes we just need a little organisation to encourage us to get out more. Having a pre-packed bag full of your nature study materials, or being sure that each child is equipped with wellies and a raincoat, can make that decision to head outside a bit easier.

When we had a dog, I dutifully took her out for a three-mile walk each morning. Some days the weather looked miserable, and I wouldn't normally have gone. But even if it ended up tipping it down, I always really enjoyed those walks. So just like we tell our own children, the phrase 'You'll enjoy it once you get there' is something we need to remind ourselves too when it comes to spending time outdoors.

*10) Experiences*

Finally, be sure to incorporate experiences into your life. What do I mean by that? I mean, doing things that generate special memories for yourself and your family. Experiences take a little more planning and effort, and probably involve spending a bit more money, but they enhance our lives in so many ways.

An experience could be a day trip to London, looking round an art gallery or visiting a medieval castle. It could be doing water sports, going on a hike, training for a half-marathon or booking in for a high-ropes or rock-climbing session. You could get tickets to a show, enjoy a concert or watch a play. Perhaps you could go a bit further and visit the historical sites of Rome, or volunteer for a mission trip in Africa, or even take a month off and travel around the UK in a camper van! The options are endless.

Sometimes it's all too easy to get caught up with the day-to-day, run-of-the-mill, ticking-off-your-to-do-list kind of life. Or we feel like we need to keep pressing on with the children's lessons and book work. But one of the reasons we chose to home-educate in the first place was that we valued freedom. So, make the most of that freedom and enjoy your precious time together. Live it to the full as much as possible and make memories. Take photos and talk about the fun and interesting things you've done. Build up your life experiences, both for yourself and for your children.

**Your turn**

How did you get on? Did you give yourself a score out of ten for each one? Now look at the three categories that received the lowest score. For each category, brainstorm some ideas to help you improve your self-care in that area. Then be sure to schedule in at least two of those ideas for next week. For others, you might need to start building them into your regular weekly calendar, so make a plan now for when you're going to make those happen. Finally, consider getting a self-care support buddy who can help you stay on track with your self-care goals.

Home education is a wonderful journey, but a lot relies on you, the parent. Taking time out to take care of yourself is never anything to feel guilty about. On the contrary, every member of your family will benefit from you being able to work from a place of health, rest, energy, joy and spiritual wellbeing. I wish you much health and happiness as you continue with this worthwhile endeavour!

"I have come that they may have life, and have it to the full" (John 10:10).

CHAPTER ELEVEN

# SEEKING GREEN PASTURES AND STILL WATERS: WHY SOUL CARE MATTERS FOR HOME EDUCATORS

*Alberta Stevens*

**Home education burnout is real!**
I remember it like it was yesterday: me crashed out on my living room sofa, mentally and physically exhausted, unable to muster any energy or interest in anything around me.

It was a typical June summer morning. The sun blazed into my east-facing loft windows like an unwelcome stranger. My first reaction was to pull the quilt over my head and roll over for what I hoped would be eternity, but the footsteps of my bright-eyed, bushy-tailed, early-riser nine-year-old up the stairs kept me nervously awake.

Suddenly, a foreign feeling of dread enveloped me. It wasn't just the usual 'tired mum' feeling. I had a deeper weariness at the thought of another day of extending myself. I tried to shrug it off as I got up to make my way around the house for our usual grooming, breakfast and morning-time routine. None of these familiar morning rituals brought me life. It felt like a cloud of heaviness had enshrouded me, leaving me listless and mentally passive. I tried to push myself to read, pray, scroll through social media, but nothing could shake off this intense sense of dread. It felt like my sense of taste had left my tongue and the colour had left my sight. I knew something was wrong.

My son was quickly put to task with a bag of Lego and his favourite audiobook. All I wanted to do was go back to bed. Instead, I settled for the living room sofa. This was the moment it finally dawned on me: I was completely 'burnt out'. My soul felt arid, languid and abandoned. Prior to this moment, I'd never experienced burnout in my life. This is not to say I hadn't experienced very stressful and even traumatic situations before, but this depth of listlessness was on a whole new level.

Let me be clear, I really enjoyed our first year of home education. For all intents and purposes, I was happy and content to have had the privilege of offering my son an idyllic childhood that I could have only dreamed of. I enjoyed learning alongside him, watching his curiosity and confidence blossom and the connection between us deepen.

We spent our days reading life-giving books and feasting on ideas. We sang hymns and folk songs, read aloud poetry, African fables and Western fairy tales. We learnt proverbs and idioms off by heart, in funny accents or African patois. We listened to great music and studied the life and work of great classical and culturally diverse composers. Other times, we recited notable lines from Shakespeare or Wordsworth and re-enacted the lives of British kings. We used our hands to create art at the feet of great art masters from around the world. We recorded our learning by creating wonder-full scientific experiments and models that reflected our growing understanding of the created world around us.

We took long, quiet walks to still our hearts and marvel at the playfulness of God at work in the beauty and diversity of nature. Other times, we went to art galleries, museums and historical places to bring to life what we were learning in books. At least once a week, we met up with friends in quiet or open green spaces for extended, imaginative play. We deepened our bonds with community each week going to church and doing sports like parkour, basketball and swimming.

Board games and telling each other cringeworthy jokes were our favourite ways of punctuating dull lessons. We found creative ways to learn domestic tasks like cooking, baking, cleaning and tidying up. We listened to audiobooks to make chores fun and memorable. On very cold winter evenings, we snuggled up on the sofa with hot cocoa and biscuits; listened to old-school soul and jazz or watched iconic wholesome movies to our hearts' content.

There was never a dull moment in our tiny, multi-cultural, single parent, urban, Charlotte-Mason-esque (with a dash of Classical) home school (see also Appendix A).

**How did I get here?**

So, if our home education experience was so good, what went wrong? How on earth did I get here … crashed out on a sofa, burnt out?

In a way, seeing the positive effect of home education on my son led into a vicious performance-approval cycle for me. Having made the decision to home-educate an only, yet very extroverted, child, I felt it was solely down to me to satisfy every aspect of his growth. If he was bored, lonely, sad or excitable, I felt it was my responsibility to fix. The more of his needs I met, the more motivated I felt to keep going. I was blinded to the fact that my effort to constantly fan his flames was rooted in my own need for approval and praise.

Obviously, this warped thinking gradually began to deplete my soul. I had no time for myself. My self-worth became rooted in how much I was doing for others. It took crashing on my sofa for a couple of days for the penny to drop.

For me, my first year of home-educating my son was everything I'd dreamt of doing for him and more. It delighted me to water the roots of my child's flourishing soul; but somehow, I forgot to see the withering leaves of my own.

## Mothers must go out to play

As home educators and especially mothers, we often forget that we too are 'whole persons' with fragile inner lives that need a rich daily diet of intellectual, spiritual and soul-enriching food. We spend countless days and nights agonising over how to fulfil our children's, spouse's, or friends' lives. We sometimes become so addicted to leading and serving that finding time to sit still, to hear the true murmurings of our souls, becomes like finding gold dust.

Soul keeping, or soul care, shouldn't be something we arrive at after all other boxes have been ticked. The state of our inner lives matters to God. It also dictates how we engage with and give to others. As Christian home educators who view motherhood as a ministry, modelling the life we wish for our children is imperative. Making time to replenish ourselves inwardly will allow us to serve our children from the overflow of our own well-nourished souls. It is out of this overflow that we can find joy and energy to lay a delightful and nourishing feast for our children as well as serve others.

## Mother culture, mother nurture, or scholè?

Within the home education tradition, the practice of developing the intellectual, spiritual and recreational pursuits of the educating parent is often referred to as 'mother culture' (if you're in the Charlotte Mason camp), or 'Scholè' (in the Classical camp) (see Appendix A for more information on different educational philosophies).

'Mother culture' is a Charlotte-Mason-inspired concept, made popular by Karen Andreola in the 1990s. Even though Charlotte Mason never used the phrase 'mother culture', the concept can be traced through the arc of her six volumes of work. Mason believed that mothers should have a rich intellectual, recreational and cultural life outside of educating their children. She encouraged mothers to take time to play (as in take on hobbies), read, go to galleries, or simply rest and refresh themselves. This way they are able to model the values, home culture and lifestyle that they hope to instil in their children. For example, Mason recommends that mothers read widely and stay informed so they can be an effective reference point for and facilitator of their children's learning.

Karen Andreola explains mother culture as "the skilful art of how a mother looks after the ways of her household. With a 'thinking love' she creates a culture in the home all her own. A mother does a lot of taking care, so she needs to take care of herself too. As a mother is feeding and cultivating the souls of her children, she is nourishing her own soul with ideas, while taking a little time for her own play and creativity" (2018, p.1).

'Mother nurture', a fairly new term coined by Min J Hwang from 'Lifegiving Motherhood' (a space committed to supporting the soul care of home-educating mums), makes a deeper call for the spiritual growth of mothers. Mother nurture stresses the importance of Christian home-educating mothers making time to tune in to the leadership of the Holy Spirit – who is, after all, the ultimate teacher/educator, both to mother and child. Mother nurture beckons mothers to make time for God, for creativity and for learning communities, to enable them to be life-giving to their children.

Scholè, the Greek word for 'restful learning', finds its roots within the classical home education tradition. The scholè tradition encourages mothers to pursue learning through reading a wide range of books alongside their children. Mothers are encouraged to note down their learning and build learning communities in which they can share their reflections with others.

All three of these pathways point to the need for home educators to see growing and nurturing their inner lives (be it spiritually, intellectually or artistically) as integral to offering their children a full, wholesome education. Simply put, we can't pour from empty cups. As Charlotte Mason aptly reminds us:

*"Education is a life. That life is sustained on ideas. Ideas are of spiritual origin, and God has made us so that we get them chiefly as we convey them to one another, whether by word of mouth, written page, Scripture word, musical symphony; but we must sustain a child's inner life with ideas as we sustain his body with food."* (1906, p.109)

If we believe education is a life, that suggests that education should apply to body, soul and spirit. The mind, like the body, needs nourishing food, which (as we see in the quote above) is ideas of all kinds. In essence, we must become intentional about offering our souls as broad and lavish a buffet of life-giving ideas and spiritual experiences as we offer our children.

## Practical ways to care for your soul

If you are anything like me, you're probably thinking, 'Yes, I get your point, but how do I do it in practice? What does soul care look like?' Well, I'm glad you asked, because since my sofa episode, I've spent a lot of time learning about tending the garden of my own soul, which I am now able to share with others.

Below are eight ways that home educators could invest in and nourish their own souls (they are not intended to be exhaustive). You will find some obvious overlaps with the 'self-care' tips mentioned in the previous chapter; but soul care is about more than replenishing yourself physically and emotionally: it is about investing in your own intellectual, cultural and spiritual resources, for the benefit of both yourself and your family. I have categorised the ideas below into two groups. The first covers those inspiring practices that 'breathe in' life to us, whilst the second looks at practices through which we 'breathe out' life into the world through our God-given abilities.

I find that balanced soul care needs a combination of activities from both categories. Each category feeds into the other, forming a beautiful life-giving cycle for nourishing our souls.

## Breathe in *(inhale)*

### 1. Solitude

Jesus modelled for us the importance of taking time alone. There are at least six distinct instances recorded in the Gospels wherein He took time in solitude and prayer. He did this to:

a. Prepare for a major activity (Luke 4:1-2, 14-15)

b. Restore His soul after hard work (Mark 6:30-32)

c. Process grief (Matthew 14:1-13)
d. Reflect ahead of an important decision (Luke 6:12-13)
e. Rest in the Father in a time of distress (Luke 22:39-44)
f. Pray in a focused and intense way (Luke 5:16)

It is important that parents take time alone to recalibrate, process, or just rest. Solitude – choosing to be alone for a while – is necessary if we are truly to reconnect with God and reflect on who He wants us to be. Failing to take time out from our phones, the daily hustle and chores leaves us operating as puppets to the tugs of our ego. But finding that time and opportunity is by no means an easy feat. The constant pull of a home educator's life leaves little time for finishing one's morning coffee, let alone finding time to be still. I get it. But we must find that time. Our sanity depends on it.

Some home educators are intentional about scheduling quiet time for the whole family in their days. This could be after your lessons, or before bed. Perhaps you are an early riser, so plan your alone time then. Getting time alone to calm down and process is integral to serving our families well. So do your best to make solitude the cornerstone of your daily rhythm.

*2. Prayer*

As a Christian, taking time to pause and release my anxieties and needs to God is life-giving. This happens through prayer and meditating on God's Word. Prayer not only changes things: it changes us. There is something profound in the way God reveals Himself (and our own hearts) to us in prayer. Furthermore, in prayer, we are able to surrender our longings, desires and needs (even just for a moment) to a trusted Father who, if you believe, will make everything beautiful in its time.

Prayer can be daunting for people who aren't used to it. Sometimes we just don't know what to say. Even for those who are accustomed to praying, slowing down until the cares of life subside and our hearts are genuinely opened to God can be a deep struggle. This is even more the case when we are hurried, stressed or in deep pain. These are times when we might want to borrow words that other Christians have prayed over the centuries. Use the Psalms, use liturgies, hymns, devotionals or poetry.

Prayer is not to be seen as a chore, but rather a privilege to be savoured that helps us unpack the depths of our own souls. It is that place of rest to which Jesus invites us to rest in Him.

## 3. Reading

Literature has a way of helping us transcend our current circumstances and bringing us into a terrain of hope. It instils in us wonder and imagination and reminds us to fight for our happy-ever-afters. Through books we can stand on the shoulders of giants, and travel to far-away lands and eras. Books bind together generations and diverse cultures across time. It's a no-brainer not to take time to replenish your soul with fiction, non-fiction, poetry and sacred texts.

As home educators, we are often very good at offering our children a plethora of soul-edifying books. We even go as far as reading aloud to them and spending time discussing and sharing our passion for the classics. However, making time to intentionally read books that build our own intellectual and spiritual growth can be cumbersome. Charlotte Mason encouraged mothers to read widely. Not only does this model good habits for our children; it helps to develop our own minds and hearts.

There are many ways we can circumvent the trap of busy motherhood to find time to read. Audiobooks and podcasts are certainly one of them. With audiobooks you can never be bored or lonely whilst you cook, do the laundry, or clean the house. You could also join a book club or listen to book reviews.

## 4. Finding beauty

There is something magical about our ability to perceive and appreciate beauty in nature, or in art, that revives and connects our souls with the Divine. This is one of the reasons why so many of us love to get away to beautiful, serene destinations – whether beach islands or camping – or visit cultured cities. Our desire to stand and stare – to see a beautiful garden, take a walk in the park, appreciate art, watch a good movie, go to the theatre or touch luxurious fabrics – isn't frivolous. It is as necessary to the soul as food is to the body.

Those of us who educate from a Christian perspective know how important it is to cultivate the idea of beauty in our children's minds. For this pursuit of truth, goodness and beauty to be successful, we need to cultivate beauty within and around ourselves too.

*"A man [everyone] should hear a little music, read a little poetry, and see a fine picture every day of his life, in order that worldly cares may not obliterate the sense of the beautiful which God has implanted in the human soul."* (Johann Wolfgang von Goethe as quoted in Musical Musings P.95, by Wiley F Gates, 1889.)

If you are going to spend a lot of time at home, which we do as home educators, be sure to surround yourself with beauty. Put up quotes, paintings and pictures that inspire you and communicate your family's values. You could try to bring the outside in by dotting your home with plants and flowers, if these bring you joy. Scented candles and calm music are also great ways to uplift one's spirit, as well as reading (see previous point). Set time aside to watch a good movie or go to the theatre, a gallery or garden. Sometimes just being able to spruce yourself up or put on your favourite outfit can lighten up your countenance. Finding beauty does not have to cost money; just take time to notice what inspires you and make a habit of doing it.

## 5. Learning community

In my experience, no other aspect of community typifies the gradual withering of the common life as described by Jon Yates in his book, 'Fracture', as a newcomer trying to navigate their local home education community. Many of us are unwilling to extend ourselves beyond our individual preferences, lifestyles and beliefs to form an inclusive, healthy common life. Whilst our dividing points may not be education levels or wealth as Yates argues, for us home educators it's our lifestyle choices, faith and education philosophies which sets tight boundaries around who we let into our cliques.

As challenging and emotional exhausting as this process of finding community can be, it is worth putting in time to find your tribe, the people with whom you belong. We, including our children, are social beings who thrive and grow from learning and sharing with one another. Nothing beats the spark we get from being around fellow home educators who can encourage, inspire, empathise with or challenge us towards our most excellent selves. Sometimes a virtual community may offer you more camaraderie than your local groups and if that is the case, work on building your relationships in that community. During lockdown in 2020, I created a monthly book club and led a weekly Bible study and prayer group, all of which met virtually. These communities became lifelines at the height of the pandemic and breathed much life into my soul with fresh ideas, creativity and new perspectives.

## **Breathe Out** *(Exhale)*

### *6. Creativity*

The more time we take doing the 'breathe in' practices above, the more we are likely to find the space to 'breathe out' in expressing our God-given creative abilities. "Creativity is intelligence having fun", you may have heard it said. Mothers would do well to go out and have a little intelligent fun, to paraphrase Charlotte Mason.

So, how do you express your creativity? I believe we are all creative. Some express their creativity through writing, journalling, scrapbooking, calligraphy, drawing, painting, pottery, sculpting, etc. Others try their hands at gardening, cooking, DIY, woodwork, knitting, crochet, sewing, needlework, playing music, dancing or creating beautiful spaces; the list goes on. Find something you enjoy doing that allows you to express the depths of your soul, so that like your Father in heaven, you can create beauty out of nothing or chaos. Who knows, someone might even be prepared to pay you for your craft.

*7. Atmosphere*

What we cultivate in our own physical, emotional, spiritual and psychological environment will invariably be reflected in our wider surroundings, which affects our children. This is the essence of the famous Charlotte Mason Parent Union (PNEU) motto, "Education is an atmosphere, a discipline, a life" (1906, p.426). The rhythms, habits, rituals and general ambience of your home are born out of your inner life as a parent.

It is therefore necessary that we not only rest our souls, but that we make time to fill our souls with good things so that when they overflow (and overflow it will in your home), what comes out leaves a beautiful fragrance in the atmosphere for those around us. "Out of the overflow of the heart the mouth speaks" (Luke 6:45).

*8. Self-care*

Arguably all the tips mentioned so far can be seen as 'self-care'. As the previous chapter covers a lot on looking after our bodies, I will only add these final thoughts. As parents (especially mums), allowing ourselves the occasional beauty or fashion treat can become sacrilegious when we have so much to do for the children and the home. Who wrote that script? Tear it up! Looking after yourself physically is good for your self-esteem. It is also good for our spouses, our children and the world to see us looking and feeling good about ourselves. Go on, celebrate you. You are a masterpiece! A walking, breathing piece of art!

For me, it took crashing on my sofa for two days to realise the depths of aridity in my soul. I emerged feeling humbled yet triumphant. Humbled, because I learnt all my effort to serve and sustain my family is nothing without God. Triumphant, because I felt equipped with clarity and empowered to prioritise my own education and wellbeing as just as important to God as my son's education and wellbeing is to me. To take time to feed my inner world is an act of nourishment and worship.

As Sarah MacKenzie in her book, 'Teaching from Rest' puts it, we must try to live and teach from a state of rest. By this she means, that we should start our daily home learning endeavour with an attitude of worship, resting in God's ability to lead and direct our efforts through prayer rather than relying on our own efforts. Through prayer we should ask the Holy Spirit to lead us and quiet our anxious souls every day so that we can really bless our children out of the overflow of our restful spirits rather than our expensive curriculum or well-structured lesson plans.

CONCLUSION

# UPHOLDING THE VISION

*Molly Ashton*

We've come a full circle in our voyage of exploration into the wonderful world of home education. I'm back at the Bishop's Palace, but this time summer is in full bloom, the flower beds are ablaze with golds and reds, and the immaculately mown lawns over-canopied with the multi-toned greens of the trees. The deep blue sky is clouding over intermittently with sudden bursts of rain. During the last one, we ran for shelter under the nearest boughs, and now as the sun comes out, one of my daughters is paddling barefooted in the puddles. A childhood filled with wonder, fuelled by curiosity, and undergirded with love.

**Capturing our vision**

I wonder what your thoughts have been as you've read each of the previous chapters? What has resonated most with you? I hope some questions have been answered and more generated. Like our children, we must never stop questioning. I wonder what has inspired you? What has challenged you? What has encouraged you?

Way back in the introduction, I talked about catching a vision for our family. I hope that as you've read through each of these chapters, packed with wisdom and practical advice, that a yearning and an excitement have been developing, ready to emerge as you spread your wings as a home-educating family. I'd encourage you to write down this newly formed vision; it's just a beginning, and will change and develop over the years, but having in mind where we are heading overall helps to inform both our smaller everyday decisions and our bigger ones.

For example, hospitality is something which is important to our family, and so the children have grown up helping to prepare meals and teatime treats, planning parties and welcoming friends and family into our home. I can already see the fruits of this in our older three, as they extend hospitality themselves.

However, only one of our children, our younger son, plays sport competitively at a senior level, partly I'm sure because we didn't invest time in taking them to training and matches much beyond primary football club level. We chose, instead, to go to church on a Sunday, as we felt this was important for their faith. Would our sport-loving son have achieved more on the rugby field if he'd played more matches on a Sunday? Most probably. Would he have the strong faith he has now? Maybe, or maybe not. In a similar vein, our children have travelled very little outside of the UK, but we did go to a large Christian camping festival (mud, mud and more mud ...!) every year, as we felt this was a good investment for their faith. Time will reveal whether the calls we made, the things we said 'yes' to and the things we said 'no' to, have been wise choices. We will have made mistakes, but I believe in a God who redeems (makes something good emerge from our messes) and already I see this at work in our children's lives. This gives us freedom to make the best decisions we can, knowing that if we get it wrong, it is not irredeemable.

## When the going gets tough

These pages have laid out a beautiful picture of the childhood we dream of for our own families. It is important to keep this vision alive. However, we will have seasons when it feels like an uphill struggle on a daily basis. Sleepless nights with little ones, sickness, financial pressures, relationship issues, children with additional needs … the list of cannon balls which bombard our homes is extensive. On top of that, home educating does mean we have very little child-free time in which to process what is happening, to take care of ourselves and to re-fuel. Chapters 10 and 11 give practical wisdom on how to avoid burning out, yet still these days will come.

I just want to speak briefly about these seasons, to encourage anyone presently going through a time of struggle. You are not alone. If you sometimes want to throw in the towel and walk away, you're not the first. I at least have been there. If you are in a time when you know you're on the edge, when you know you're not staying well regulated, when your children's behaviour seems, or is, unreasonable, I too have been there. If you wake up some mornings wondering if you have the energy to go through the day, if you feel close to tears and feel you are letting your children down, I've been there too.

It's in these seasons when, for me, my faith in God and my belief that home education is God's calling for our family, is what keeps me going. It doesn't mean I feel happy; it doesn't mean the situations are quickly fixed. However, it's where I get the strength to keep going, to keep putting one foot in front of the other. My quiet morning times are where I daily refill, in prayer, in Scripture and in a few moments of peace. Whether you have a faith or not, I urge you to incorporate a time of quiet into your lives. In the summer I sit on our front porch, in the winter on my rocking chair with a candle; always with a steaming mug of tea. We then make it through to lunch time, after which we all have a quiet time in our own rooms. This has been such a good habit for the children that the older ones continued it well into their college years on home study days. Again, it gives time for me to breathe. So, there is hope!

## Bastles

The other factor which keeps me plodding along this trajectory is my strong conviction in the importance of the family unit, not only for now, but as I look to the future.

On our recent summer holiday to Northumberland, my map-loving husband noticed many notations on his ordnance survey map, marked 'bastle'. In the true spirit of a home-educating family on holiday, we set about discovering what these buildings were all about. We learned that during the disputes between the English and Scottish Crowns in the sixteenth century, these border lands were, in the words of one museum guide we met, "like the Wild West". Raiders from the north clashed with rebels from the south and those trying to eke out an existence in the middle were often attacked and pillaged.

As a defence against this, they built fortified farmhouses, with walls up to a metre thick, where the animals sheltered on the ground floor and the family lived on the floor above. They were often positioned in small communities, and in places where they had good vantage points of the surrounding countryside, in order to see attackers before they arrived.

These homes spoke to me very poignantly about the purpose of our homes in the twenty-first century, and thus too about the significance of home education. We are living in a time of unprecedented pressure on the family unit, from the legal standing of marriage through to the insidious cultural agenda which undermines traditional family values, and the constant pressures of work, social media, screens and general busyness with sap our time and drain our energy.

There seems to be, at the root of this, a rising agenda of cultural Marxism, which very intentionally aims both to break down the family unit, acknowledged as one of the main building blocks of society, and to destroy religion, seen as giving hope and a moral framework. As we all know, education is not neutral, and in order to instil this new framework into each mind, education is key. Thus, over the second half of the twentieth century, our traditional Judeo-Christian foundation for education in the UK has been gradually replaced by a Marxist/socialist ideology, impacting universities, teacher training colleges and eventually all state education (Rose, 2016). This strategic spread has been so effective that, I would suggest, it has infiltrated many of our mindsets without us even noticing. The analogy of a frog slowly being heated up in a tank of water seems apt; it's not until the water is boiling and the frog is about to die that it notices the gradual increase in temperature.

As a Christian, I strongly believe that we need to be teaching our young children a biblical worldview. I question the current philosophy of exposing children to as wide a variety of ideologies and choices as one can muster. I explained in the introduction how bank tellers are taught to recognise false notes by initially handling as many true ones as possible. Similarly, we develop our children's palates by giving them small amounts of wholesome food as we wean them. We don't bombard them with junk food, waiting until the appropriate ages to expose them to this. In the same way, I have become convinced that we need to do all in our power to ensure our children are taught in their early years from a biblical foundation.

As you're reading this book, home education is probably the route you are on. However, as I mentioned in the introduction, there are a small but steadily increasing number of independent Christian schools throughout the UK, which also teach children from a biblical worldview. Some work in partnership with home-educating families, having been begun by home educators themselves. I believe that as Christian parents, we need to work alongside each other as we endeavour to bring our children up according to God's good laws, and suggest that both home educators and Christian schools can draw from each other's strengths to mutual benefit in our joint cause.

In his most recent book, Rod Dreher (2020) explains the current rise of 'soft totalitarianism', fuelled by a religious fervour for Marxist ideology. He offers suggestions as to how we can resist it, gleaned from families who survived the 'hard' totalitarianism of communism during the twentieth century. Strong families, and a faith for which many were prepared to be tortured, imprisoned or even to die, were key. This type of family unit and unshakable faith does not happen by chance. It involved intentional investment by many parents. Most children had to attend state schooling, which was fundamental in producing good citizens – loyal to the state above all else. So, parents had to be committed to counteracting this mindset at home.

Dreher relates the incredible story of the large Benda family who lived in Prague. Both parents, who were academics, worked at the topmost level of the Czech dissident movement and suffered greatly for their faith, including imprisonment. Vaclav Benda believed that "the family is the bedrock of civilisation and must be nurtured and protected at all costs" (p.130). He saw both the threat which communism posed to the family and the role the traditional family could take in Christian resistance. They had numerous strategies for preparing and training their children to stand firm. One of these was reading aloud; Kamila Benda read for three hours to their children when they returned home from school, including 'The Lord of the Rings' three times ... for them, Mordor was real. Other strategies I picked up from this book were the importance of community and small groups, the preservation of cultural memory (become a second-hand book squirrel, as I suggested in the introduction, and read to your children), and the need to be constantly striving for truth.

I believe that home-educating our children is an essential way to build and preserve strong families. As we seem to be living in an ever-increasing swirl of confusion and disorder, we are still able to craft our homes into places of refuge and sanctuary, places of hearty mealtime discussions and family bonding and laughter, places where stories are read, music is played, and beautiful art is displayed on the walls. Our homes can be places where others come to find warmth and grace, and from which we gradually send our children out to be bearers of hope, in the knowledge that we have done all we can to enable them to stand strong in the face of storms to come.

I would like to add that if, after reading this book, you do not feel home education is the right route for you, please be encouraged that you can, like the Benda family, have a home filled with good books and stirring conversations, with laughter and love, as you intentionally seek after truth and invest in your family. Be encouraged and inspired by families such as these.

Back to bastles. While none of us now live in buildings with metre-thick walls and a cow in the basement (though please let us know if you do!), I believe they have a significance for our time about the need to protect all that is good and true, to live in community with others and to be ever-vigilant for what spiritual assaults might be coming our way.

**Laying the foundations of the next generation**

I've loved reading each and every chapter of this book and am so grateful for the authors who have shared wisdom, expertise, experience, passion and vulnerability. Home education involves courage, faith, sacrifice and sheer grit at times, but the rewards are sweet in the everyday, the longer term and eternity. I now have a good number of home-educating friends who, like us, have their eldest children in further education. It is not surprising that we speak longingly of the days when all our children were at home; when we all piled in the car together and went on an adventure; when we all snuggled around with mugs of hot chocolate and listened to a read-aloud; when we all shared in the fun of Christmas parties and sports days.

Maybe our vision has become a little misty as we glance back fondly, but as I look at these young adults now, I can only be amazed and deeply humbled at their strength of character, their convictions, their compassion and their desire to walk in their God-given callings. They are all uniquely different. Life has not been easy for many; home-educating our children is not a fail-safe that prevents them from having to walk through difficult, challenging and sometimes heart-wrenchingly painful seasons. But, from my observations, they are well equipped to do so. They are only like this due to the intentional decisions and sacrificial love of their parents.

So, in concluding, I would like to honour and applaud all those families who have walked this path and seen their carefree children emerge as strong and competent young adults. I would like to pour a cup of tea and serve up some delicious cake to those of you living through the ups and downs of home education life at the moment. I'm sure you could do with a few minutes' peace. And I'd like to encourage those of you looking from the brink, to take this step of faith and begin to walk on water.

May we all know God's provision, protection and peace as we boldly and faithfully lay the foundations of the next generation.

*Afterword*

# "NO! THESE ARE OUR SONS AND DAUGHTERS."

*Randall and Mary Hardy*

What an inspiring read this has been – encouraging, honest, practical and challenging all at once. A great summary of many of the issues faced by parents who have opted for this particular 'road less travelled', and such a compilation of accumulated wisdom and experience that there remains little for us to say.

Several contributors have touched on what one might call the timeless elements that underpin many of our common endeavours, factors such as the importance of family relationships, the transmission of values, and a whole-life approach to learning. Because these are based on personal conviction, for most of us these would hopefully remain with us as fundamentals no matter what external conditions we had to operate under as home educators in future.

On the other hand, we would be naïve not to acknowledge that our home education takes place against the backcloth of life as it is playing out in the here and now. Our home educating component doesn't exist independently in a time-warp or bubble. We have to raise our children by our example so they know how to be overcomers in their own generation, rather than in the context in which we grew up – which may feel very distant now. We ourselves need to live by a world-view which will equip them to do this.

Awareness of living in a rapidly changing society was noted by several writers, and it is our conviction that things are getting harder and will continue to do so. We desperately need an understanding of the times, and to consider the issue of our freedom to home educate against the bigger picture of what is happening in our society. There is a pressing need to discern what the Lord is doing through those events. We mustn't isolate one from the other.

In reviewing the chapters, one matter was conspicuous by its absence, and it's one frequently overlooked by home educating parents. Something of an elephant in the room maybe, rarely addressed until there's a crisis. Overlooked partly due to the pressures of day to day living, partly because it's hard to understand, perhaps because it's not nice to sense that some ill-defined threat may be overshadowing our home education endeavours. You've guessed – the matter of politics and how the direction of travel in Westminster and the other seats of devolved government affects our ongoing freedom to home educate our children.

**A wake-up call**

We were both born in the early 1950s, an era where very different values and an opposite world-view prevailed, at least superficially. As already noted, the intervening years have seen significant changes of attitude in society, in people's general perceptions of life, and most particularly in their expectations and concept of the role of the state in the lives of its citizens.

Neither of us really had time or inclination to take much notice of what was going on in the world of politics when our children were young, but the infamous Badman Review of 2009/10 proved something of a wake-up call for us both. Never had we expected to find ourselves collecting local signatures for a petition, or going to London to meet our MP and lobby Parliament along with other home educators from right across the spectrum. But there was something worrying about the way politicians and children's professionals had begun to speak of children as though they no longer belonged to their parents. Somehow as parents we intuitively felt a need for pushback, a response of, "No, these are our children."

Of course there was widespread relief when the proposals about registration and monitoring of home educated children intended for inclusion in the Children Schools & Families Bill were dropped in the run-up to the 2010 General Election. But it was clear to anyone with eyes to see that these issues were not going to go away. The watchman must remain vigilant, with his eye on the distant horizon, warning of continuing danger.

And so began our journey of learning the jargon and procedures of how the parliamentary system works, and understanding more about political agendas and the threat to HE freedom. Mary recalls being challenged back in the early 90s by a speaker's closing words at a home educators' conference at Cliff College. "Celebrate your freedom!" he urged, and this resonated ever more clearly with us as we came to realise that home education freedoms were a contested matter, one which parents could not and should not take for granted.

**Ongoing hostility**

In 2017 the heat was turned up again, with early signs of a return to hostilities; then came Lord Soley's full-on attack with his Private Member's Home Education (Duty of Local Authorities) Bill. All this accompanied by an increasingly hostile media environment which saw home education unjustifiably associated with a range of societal ills such as being radicalised, abused or trafficked.

Whatever we as individuals may have experienced in the way of adverse reaction to our non-standard educational choices is also reflected more broadly in the way that blame for a whole range of problems and difficulties gets laid at the door of home educators en masse.

The long-standing negative media narrative has done no favours to the public's perception of such matters. Fear-mongering and the use of emotive language have successfully convinced the average person of two things: that "a child in school is safe," and that those being educated by their family are "in need of safeguarding." Not so by any means, as we well know. In actual fact, many of the issues reported concern problems which are endemic to the school system – but the prevailing message still does its work.

**Getting to the root of the matter**

Gradually we were coming to see that a larger root cause lay behind or beyond what we had taken to be 'the problem.' Some readers may recall an illustration used by Randall in a conference session he took in 2020. He used the analogy of catching different sizes of ball. A cricket ball – easy ... a basketball – easy ... a giant beach ball – possibly. But as the size of what needed catching grew larger and larger, the task became daunting to the point of impossibility. Who would not feel intimidated by the thought of trying to get their arms around something so much larger and heavier than they had ever anticipated?

It was becoming apparent to us that the ongoing issues commonly faced by home educators (such as dealing with a difficult LA staff member, an unsympathetic LA department or an unhelpful MP) were an expression of a more far-reaching agenda.

The national misinformation campaign grew, drawing on pre-existing bias or negative attitudes within government about alternative forms of education in general. In fact these two were resulting in something of a feedback loop. While parliamentary questions and lobbyists kept up the pressure for something to be done about 'the problem of home education,' consultation responses from official bodies and international organisations began to reveal the broader agenda.

The influence was not going from the bottom up, but coming from the top down, we realised. We saw that the roots of the adverse messaging about family were both transnational and long-standing. Recent decades have seen the flourishing of an emphasis on children's rights. In fact, children are now portrayed as independent rights-bearing citizens, and the state as the agent with the duty to protect children from their parents usurping those rights. This sleight of hand may not be easy to recognise, but it concerns the application of negative human rights as though they were positive ones. Negative rights were developed in order to prevent states from withholding provisions such as education from any of their citizens. However, the message has increasingly morphed into a demand that these rights be positively applied, thereby justifying the state's intervention into and oversight of citizens' and in particular families' private lives.

The current expression of this ideology may be seen in the conflation of education and welfare, as expressed through the increased appeal to safeguarding. In respect to home education, this is driving the demand for governments to define exactly what constitutes 'a suitable education.' No longer are our children viewed by the powers that be merely as members of individual families – they are global citizens, and the responsibility of shaping the thinking of the rising generation rests with the state. In the context of this big state mentality, parental choice becomes a difficult issue.

"Real people out there living outside of the school system," was the way Siân Lowe chose to describe the home educators she had met at the start of her journey. And unwittingly she may have expressed the nub of the political problem here because, as she so rightly observed, "When you step outside of the norm, it can be unsettling not just for you, but for those around you as well."

To put it in the simplest terms – proactive home educators who aim to raise their children to be capable, independent, thinking adults unsettle the system. States much prefer an inclusive one-size-fits-all educational approach with passive, compliant parents who appreciate someone else doing their thinking for them.

You may have spotted an anti-family tone in policy areas other than education. You may have noticed how influential opinion-formers in the world of education or children's services are prone to speak of our children. You may have had vague reservations about the superficially laudable Sustainable Development Goals, wondering if there might be a sub-plot about the shaping of young minds to conform to a pre-determined agenda. Much of this can be traced back to organisations such as UNESCO and UNICEF. The objective of the monoculture behind this agenda was articulated very clearly by the first Director of UNESCO, prominent humanist Julian Huxley, in his 1946 document, "UNESCO Its Purpose and Its Philosophy."

**Where do we go from here?**

The boundaries of local and even national struggles are dwarfed by the larger parameters of a global agenda involving children and education. The skills and tools for fighting 'yesterday's war' will need reviewing and upgrading if parents are to stand their ground in this bigger arena.

Our encouragement therefore to today's home educating parents must be to wield both trowel and sword, continuing to build good things into their children's lives, but at the same time making realistic preparations to play their part in protecting the family unit from 'big state incursion' into the lives of ordinary families.

The agenda is now so far-reaching, it will not be quelled by a few activists. We live in times when the reach of the state into the life of the private citizen is being extended on multiple fronts. Civil liberties have clearly been under assault in recent years. The present challenges need everyone in the HE communities on board, not just some of them. Co-ordinated responses to government consultations or proposals have their place, but in one way this is a little people's war, with the outcome dependent on each family's level of determination to push back and reassert the natural and historic boundaries of their God-given remit.

The Barbers were spot on when they wrote about most parents having unwittingly handed over a privilege and a responsibility that belongs to them. Charles' closing words about Dads rising to their God-given role of preparing and training their children for adulthood are the outcome of a change of heart about this. Equally, fathers need to take the lead in their families' response to the ubiquitous onslaught on family-based education. We note that the project to rebuild the wall of Jerusalem was completed effectively and in a very short time because each family repaired a section adjacent to their own home.

There is no place for complacency. Christian home educating parents need to value their responsibilities to the LORD, and the civil liberties which allow them to fulfil these, sufficiently to take both seriously. If not, He would in no way be unjust to allow the removal of our current liberties.

## A call to arms

Don't spend your time looking back nostalgically. Don't be an ostrich either. Rather, whenever it is that you read this, pray urgently for an understanding of the times in which you are living, and the wisdom to respond appropriately.

This is important, because if our prayers are to be effective, they need to be aligned to His will. Be aware of our human tendency to pray according to our own wills, especially where we have much invested. (As American author Rod Dreher discovered, some Christian parents have had to continue raising their children in the fear of the Lord in much more hostile regimes than we presently experience.)

Observe, listen and read as widely as you can about what is going on in the world of education and about the philosophies being pursued by educationalists and children's professionals. Try to keep abreast of what is being said by politicians and in the media, using sites which pre-digest or summarise material if you have limited time available.

Besides clarifying your own family's vision and values as recommended earlier, think hard about the God-given primacy of parents in preparing children for their futures, and contrast this with the purposes of state education to train children to fit into the world's mould. Where are the boundaries between these two? The real threat is being driven by an ubiquitous ideology that seeks to reidentify your sons and daughters collectively as *their children*.

Engagement by consulting with your political representatives, such as saying no to registration, or writing to the press, becomes easier once you've identified some core issues and thought about them sufficiently to know what you want to say. Find those who are working next to you, and look for ways of supporting one another.

Standing against this ideology requires courage, but there are few things more determined than parents galvanised into defending their young. This is not simply about protecting the right to home educate: it is about protecting the responsibility of parents to be parents.

It behoves us all to remember the insightful words of Lady Hales from the 2016 Supreme Court's judgment on the Scottish Named Person Scheme:

*"The first thing that a totalitarian regime tries to do is to get at the children, to distance them from the subversive, varied influences of their families, and indoctrinate them in their rulers' view of the world. Within limits, families must be left to bring up their children in their own way."* [Para.73]

## *Appendix A*
# EDUCATIONAL PHILOSOPHIES

*Juliet English*

Because of the freedom which we enjoy in the UK, you have options as to how you approach your child's education. The approach you choose will depend on your own philosophy on childhood and education, your family's lifestyle, your child's personality, temperament and needs, and other factors. Some parents may start out with one approach, and then adapt and change as they become more comfortable or find a way that works better for their family. It is important to find something that works for you. The following are five popular approaches that parents might choose to follow in the UK – however, there are a great many other variations and combinations of these.

### Traditional / structured approach

This approach generally entails using graded textbooks or workbooks which follow a scope and sequence in each subject in progressive increments. They may include teachers' manuals, tests and record-keeping materials, and assume that education will resemble that of a school classroom.

The student will follow a set programme of learning lessons, completing assignments and testing before moving on to the next section. A set programme allows for minimal preparation and supervision on the part of the parent, and is based on a lot of independent study.

*Strengths:*

- Everything is laid out for ease of use
- Follows a standardised scope and sequence
- Has definite milestones of accomplishment
- Testing and grading are easy to do

*Weaknesses:*

- Is geared to the 'generic' child, not taking into account individual learning styles, strengths and weaknesses, or interests
- Assumes that there is a body of information that comprises an education and that this information can be broken down into daily increments
- Treats children's minds like containers to be filled with information
- Focuses on transmitting information through artificial learning experiences
- Is teacher-directed and blackboard-oriented
- Different aged students study different materials
- Expensive when teaching multiple children
- Discourages original, independent thinking
- Has a high 'burnout' rate

**The classical approach**

This approach to education has produced great minds throughout history. The modern proponent of the classical approach was British writer and medieval scholar Dorothy Sayers. As the Nazis rose to power in the 1930s, Sayers warned that schools were teaching children everything except how to think. Because young adults could no longer think for themselves, Sayers felt they could easily be influenced by whatever tyrant came along. To remedy this, Sayers proposed reinstating the classical form of education used in the Middle Ages.

In the classical approach, children under age 18 are taught tools of learning collectively known as *the Trivium*. The Trivium has three parts, each part corresponding to a childhood developmental stage.

The first stage of the Trivium, the *Grammar Stage*, covers early elementary ages and focuses on reading, writing and spelling; the study of Latin; and developing observation, listening and memorisation skills. The goal of this stage is to master the elements of language and develop a general framework of knowledge.

The next stage, the *Dialectic Stage*, is introduced when children begin to demonstrate independent or abstract thought (usually by becoming argumentative or opinionated). The child's tendency to argue is moulded and shaped by teaching logical discussion, debate, and how to draw correct conclusions and support them with facts. The goal of this stage is to equip the child with language and thinking skills capable of detecting fallacies in an argument. Latin study is continued, with the possible addition of Greek. The student reads essays, arguments and criticisms instead of literature, as in the Grammar Stage. History study leans toward interpreting events. Higher mathematics might be introduced as well.

The final phase of the Trivium, the *Rhetoric Stage*, seeks to produce a student who can use language, both written and spoken, eloquently and persuasively. Students are usually ready for this stage by age 15.

*Strengths:*

- Is tailored to stages of mental development
- Teaches thinking skills and verbal/written expression
- Creates self-learners
- Has produced great minds throughout history

*Weaknesses:*

- Very little prepared curricula available
- Requires a scholarly teacher and student
- May overemphasise ancient disciplines and classics

**The unit study approach**

A unit study is taking a theme or topic (a unit of study) and delving into it deeply over a period of time, integrating language, science, geography, history, maths and arts as they apply. Instead of studying eight or ten separate, unrelated subjects, all subjects are blended together and studied around a common theme or project. For example, a unit study on birds could include reading and writing about birds, and about famous ornithologists (language), studying the parts, functions and life cycles of birds, and perhaps even the aerodynamics of flight (science and mathematics), determining the migration paths, habitats and ecological/sociological impact of birds (geography, environmental studies), sketching familiar birds (art), building bird houses or feeders ('hands-on' activities) and so forth. This is similar to project-based learning, and tools such as lapbooking work well with unit studies.

*Strengths:*

- All ages can learn together
- Children can delve as deeply into a subject as they like
- The family's interests can be pursued
- Students get the whole picture
- Curiosity and independent thinking are generated
- Intense study of one topic is the more natural way to learn
- Knowledge is interrelated so is learned easily and remembered longer
- Unit studies are fairly easy to create

### Weaknesses:

- It is easy to leave educational 'gaps'
- Hard to assess the level of learning occurring
- Record keeping may be difficult
- Prepared unit study curricula are expensive
- Do-it-yourself activities require planning
- Too many activity-oriented unit studies may cause burnout for the parent and child
- Subjects that are hard to integrate into the unit may be neglected

**The 'living books' / Charlotte Mason approach**

The 'living books' approach is based on the writings of Charlotte Mason, who was a British educator at the turn of the twentieth century. Miss Mason was appalled by several tendencies she noticed in modern education:

1. The tendency to treat children as containers to be filled with pre-digested information, instead of as human beings
2. The tendency to break down knowledge into thousands of isolated bits of information to be fed into 'container' children
3. The tendency to engineer artificial learning experiences

She believed in respecting children as persons, in involving them in real-life situations, and in allowing them to read really good books, instead of what she called "twaddle" (1886, p.205) – worthless, inferior teaching material. She considered education a failure when it produced children able to "do harder sums and read harder books" but who lacked "moral and ... intellectual power" (1886, p.99). Children were to be taught good habits, involved in a broad spectrum of real-life situations and given ample time to play and create.

Mason's approach to academics was to teach basic reading, writing and mathematics skills, then expose children to the best sources of knowledge for all other subjects. This meant giving children experiences like nature walks, observing and collecting wildlife, visiting art museums, and reading real books with 'living ideas'. She called such books "living books" (1886, p.7) because they made the subject 'come alive', unlike books that tend to be dry and dull and assume the reader cannot think for him/herself.

*Strengths:*

- Treats children as active participants in the learning process
- Exposes children to the best sources of knowledge – real objects and books instead of second-hand interactions with distilled information
- Encourages curiosity, creative thinking and a love of learning
- Eliminates meaningless tasks or busywork
- Stresses formation of good character and habits

*Weaknesses:*

- Tends to be very child-centred
- Very little prepared curricula
- May neglect higher level studies because of its emphasis on art, literature and nature study
- May become too eclectic

**The 'unschooling' approach**

This approach was defined by John Holt, a twentieth-century educator who concluded that children have an innate desire to learn and a curiosity that drives them to learn what they need to know when they need to know it. Holt believed that both desire and curiosity are destroyed by the usual methods of teaching. In his book, 'Teach your Own', Holt wrote: "What children need is not new and better curricula but access to more and more of the real world; plenty of time and space to think over their experiences and to use fantasy and play to make meaning out of them; and advice, road maps, guidebooks to make it easier for them to get where they want to go (not where we think they ought to go), and to find out what they want to find out" (Holt and Farenga, 2021, p.50/31).

On the other hand, 'unschooling' refers to any less structured learning approach that allows children to pursue their own interests with parental support and guidance, and lets children learn by being included in the life of adults. The child is surrounded by a rich environment of books, learning resources and adults who model a lifestyle of learning and are willing to interact with him/her. Formal academics, if pursued at all, are pursued when the need arises, and normally as desired by the child in their personal learning journey. In this approach children are 'apprenticed' by adults who include them in what they are doing. In the process, the child learns everything the adult knows and possibly a good deal more. Parents may facilitate by connecting the child to resources that allow them to progress in subjects that interest them.

*Strengths:*

- Takes little planning
- Captures the child's 'teachable moments'
- Children have access to the real world, and plenty of time and space to figure things out on their own
- Children are less likely to become academically frustrated or 'burnt out'
- Children can delve into a subject as deeply as desired
- Creates self-learners with a love of learning

### Weaknesses:

- Very unstructured
- May neglect some subjects
- Hard to assess level of learning
- Lacks the security of a clearly laid-out curriculum
- Is extremely child-centred
- Difficult to explain to others

## *Appendix B*
# PRACTICAL ADVICE ON RUNNING A HOME EDUCATION SUPPORT GROUP

*Juliet English*

**What do I need to start a home education support group?**
If you only know a handful of other home educators, don't be put off. A good way to approach it is to plan activities that you and your children would enjoy doing anyway and invite others to join you. That way, even if initially it is just your family, you need not be discouraged, but if others do join you, it's a bonus!

Two to three families is a quite normal size for a group just starting out. Set up a Facebook page and with a bit of word of mouth, you'll be on your way!

Small groups don't normally need too much to make them work and can meet in different homes or at a park or museum initially. Keep it simple and manageable until it becomes necessary to accommodate more people in a more organised fashion.

As your group grows, you may eventually decide to investigate hiring a hall on a regular basis, splitting the costs between the participating families. A home education group can also qualify for school discounts at attractions and historic sites, if they book as an educational group.

## How to run a successful home education support group

If you are starting the support group, it is very much your prerogative to make decisions about how the group will be run. Obviously, it's wise to consider the feelings of those you might want to attract to the group, and a group run on a more consensual model will encourage members to take ownership of the group and help run it.

A person with high energy might want to take individual responsibility for organising everything but, generally, sharing the load benefits everyone. It also helps ensure the continuity of the group to have more than one person involved in the planning. A strong team makes for a strong group that will continue long after individuals have moved on.

You may want to start off with just one monthly meeting or field trip initially and adapt that later according to the needs of the group and how well it is going. Meeting for about 1.5-2 hours is normally adequate but, once again, this can be adapted to suit the group.

It's important to establish what your group's aims will be, as that will help to shape the form the group will take.

If doing hall meetings, it's helpful to have a theme to work around. There are many good ideas out there, and the possibilities really are endless. You could structure your sessions around a themed talk, and then have some organised activities which will help the children to consolidate their learning.

Do plan to have refreshments (coffee, tea, squash, biscuits, etc.) available at least once during the meeting. You may also choose to have lunch together, either as part of your meeting, or afterwards.

Most groups these days make extensive use of social media to communicate with their members. A 'closed' Facebook group is the best format to use, as administrators can ensure that anyone wanting to join is vetted by a process of their choosing, thus protecting the privacy of members. Content posted onto the group page can also be moderated, to keep it relevant to the group.

## Ideas for themed meetings

- STEM (Science, Technology, Engineering, Mathematics) themes: Learn about electricity, chemistry, mechanics, etc.

- History themes: Choose a specific period or event in history, and look at things like dress, food, weapons, transport, or government of that period.

- Food-related themes: Make your own pizza, plants as food, historic foods – there's always a way to bring food into your themes!

- Geography themes: 'Around the World', where each family picks a country and does a presentation. Each child can get a 'passport' to be stamped for each 'country' (presentation table) they visit. Rivers and waterways studies, which can include outdoor activities such as pond-dipping and boat trips. Different types of climate, weather, etc.

- Lego clubs: Have one family provide the Lego (you don't want to get different lots mixed up) and suggest themes or challenges for children to build around.

- Arts and Crafts: Themes (as above) can include craft activities, but you may wish to have dedicated art or craft meetings.

- Speakers/presentations: There are many organisations, museums, interest groups, etc., who will be more than happy to visit your group to do a talk or presentation, if you feel like this would benefit the group. It's also a really good way of educating your visitors about home education!

The possibilities really are infinite, and you can poll your group to find out what they'd be most interested in. You may have some creative members who will always offer fresh ideas and suggestions. Pinterest is also a really good source of ideas for activities and crafts.

## Practical ideas for growing a stronger community

Here are some practical ideas for helping your group grow into a vibrant, active and supportive community:

- At the beginning of each meeting, provide an introduction session where each family can say something about themselves – name, number of children and ages, where they live – so that parents can find and connect with others who have something in common.
- Take care of each other: Arrange a rota of meals provided to families where mum is unwell, or a new baby has arrived. Help each other out with childcare when needed, throw a baby shower, or help with transport to group outings.
- Encourage meet-ups outside of the group meetings – mums' nights out, picnics in the park, birthday parties – these all give opportunities for families to get to know each other better.
- Sports days: Organise fun sports days in the warmer weather.
- Christmas events: Organise a special celebration with your group, such as a Christmas dinner, or concert/nativity play, or carols by candlelight. Children can be involved in the planning of the event.
- Family camp: Book a campsite during the week in term-time (discounted rates!) for members to camp together. Activities can be organised for the camp, and many friendships will be forged as you sing around the campfire and toast marshmallows!
- End of academic year event: Hold an awards evening, where parents can recognise their children's progress. It's a good idea to limit certificates to two per child, or you could end up with a long, drawn-out event! It's also wise to discourage 'prizes' such as expensive gifts at this event, as children might perceive this as unfair. Simple certificates acknowledging that the child has achieved progress in academics, sports, character development, or other skills, is more than sufficient. It can be fun to combine this with a BBQ or shared meal for all the families.

**Some other tips:**

Keep an attendance record: This helps you to get a picture of who attends regularly, as well as average numbers to be catered for. Ask for the name of the family and ages of children.

Buy a cash box: Fees for attending the group should be sufficient to cover hall hire, materials and refreshments. You can set a different rate for single-child families and larger families, as well as discounted rates for paying for the whole term, as opposed to 'pay as you go'.

Delegate! Groups function well when the load is spread. Get other parents to assist with supervising activities and providing refreshments. Recognise individual strengths and talents and put them to good use!

If funds allow (and they should!) be sure to reimburse others for any expenses incurred, as long as they are reasonable and receipts are provided. Any large expenditures should be agreed with those involved in planning and should only be for things that will benefit the whole group.

Resolve issues with kindness. As groups get larger, there are bound to be problems and disagreements at times. Most of the time these can be resolved by speaking directly with the parties concerned, but try to avoid a 'knee-jerk' reaction, as most problems occur as the result of simple misunderstanding. It's important to be clear on the facts and not react emotionally. Also, remember that sometimes written communication (such as text messages or Facebook posts) can be misconstrued, so wording should be chosen carefully. If any group members still choose to leave as a result, it's better if they do so on amicable terms.

*Appendix C*
# HELPFUL RESOURCES

### Courses and Curriculum

Accelerated Christian Education • *teach-at-home.org*

Ambleside Online • *amblesideonline.org*

Classical Conversations • *classicalconversations.co.uk*

Dreaming Spires Home Learning • *dreamingspireshomelearning.com*

ECHO Education • *echo.education*

Exploring Nature with Children • *raisinglittleshoots.com/buy-exploring-nature-with-children*

Homegrown Sonshine: • *homegrownsonshine.co.uk*

Meet the Artists • *meettheartistsfamily.co.uk/home*

Modern Miss Mason • *leahboden.com*

NSWLearning • *nswlearning.org*

Poetry teatime • *poetryteatime.com*

Sonlight • *sonlight.com*

Streams Education • *streams.education*

## General Support for Home Education

Christian Education Europe • *christian.education*

Christian Home Education Support Service (CHESS) • *chessuk.org*

Christian Unschooling • *christian-unschooling.com*

Education Otherwise • *educationotherwise.org*

Streams • *educationstreams.education*

The HE Byte • *he-byte.uk*

## Podcasts

Mended Teacups Home Ed Podcast • *mendedteacups.wordpress.com*

Modern Miss Mason • *leahboden.com*

Readaloud Revival • *readaloudrevival.com/podcasts*

Sally Clarkson • *sallyclarkson.com*

## Exam Information and Courses

Catherine Mooney Tutoring • *catherinemooneytutoring.co.uk*

Dreaming Spires Home Learning • *www.dreamingspireshomelearning.com*

ECHO education • *echo.education*

HE Exams • *he-exams.fandom.com/wiki/HE_Exams_Wiki*

NSWLearning • *nswlearning.org*

## Special Needs Support

Christian Occupational Therapy Support • *chots.co.uk*

Home Educating a Sensory Child – with Ease: The Ultimate Guide • *Book on amazon.co.uk*

Online (non-faith based) OT Sensory Processing support • *sensoryprocessing.co.uk*

Anne Laure Jackson (YouTube) • *youtube.com/channel/UCxHPd2SseD_OrdeI9UL45zA*

## Christian Schools

ACE Christian Schools • *christian.education*

Christian Schools Trust • *christianschoolstrust.co.uk*

New Christian Schools • *newchristianschools.org*

OSCAR • *oscar.org.uk/resources/uk-schools*

## Blogs

Christian Occupational Therapy Support • *chots.co.uk*

Learn What You Live • *learnwhatyoulive.com*

Mothering Through the Seasons • *motheringthroughtheseasons.com*

Sally Clarkson • *sallyclarkson.com*

## Conferences

Learn Free • *learnfree.org.uk*

The Modern Miss Mason conference • *leahboden.com/conference*

# *Author Biographies*

**Molly Ashton (BN Hons, RGN)**

Molly is an enthusiastic advocate for home education with a passion to encourage others on this journey. She and her husband have four children, two by birth and two by adoption. Through both professional and personal experience, she has insight into the challenges of parenting children with additional needs. She co-hosts 'Mended Teacups', a UK home-education podcast, blogs at *motheringthroughtheseasons.com* and has authored one children's book. She is rooted in the beauty and rhythms of the countryside in which she and her family live in their ongoing quest towards self-sufficiency.

**Charles (MA) & Ruth Barber**

Charles and Ruth live in Bradford, West Yorkshire. Charles studied Organic Chemistry at Cambridge, has been a Christian minister and more recently worked as a trainer in adult social care. He continues to help lead and teach at Cedar Tree Church. Ruth has a background in banking and worked at Christians Against Poverty as a debt counsellor. She is now the administrator for CHESS, the Christian Home Education Support Service, recently helping to organise a national online conference for home educators. They have seven children, six boys and a girl, who have all been home-educated. The eldest three are now at university and the youngest is 12.

**Helen Brunning (BA Hons)**

Helen has been home-educating since her first child was born in 2000. She's a founder member of a local Christian home education support group and also loves teaching her own and other children in a home education co-operative group. She's keen to encourage other families in their education journey and is committed to the idea that there's a style to suit everyone's individual circumstance. She's also one half of the 'Mended Teacups' podcast team.

### Jessica Girard (Cert. Health and Social care, Cert. Theology)

Jessica Girard is the voice behind The Open Home, a blog about home education and family life on the small island of Guernsey. With a background in social work and a heart for foster care, Jessica is passionate about protecting childhood and creating a nurturing home life for the children entrusted to her care. She is married to her childhood sweetheart, David, and together they have three young children, two girls and a boy.

### Dr Kat Patrick (PhD, PGCE)

Dr Kat Patrick has home-educated her four children for almost two decades now, two of whom are at university and two in secondary. Because she grew up and studied in the US before living most of her adult life in Oxfordshire as a teacher and UK examiner, she has always been passionate about underpinning a child's studies with a broad, liberal arts education. Not only has she spoken on this topic on numerous podcasts and at conferences, she founded a tutorial company in 2012 called Dreaming Spires Home Learning, through which she and her nine colleagues offer parents a range of delight-directed options, supporting teens with their passions while ticking exam boxes if they so wish *(www.dreamingspireshomelearning.com)*.

### Juliet English (BA Social Work)

Juliet is an experienced home educator who is passionate about encouraging and empowering parents to educate their children with boldness and freedom. She has been married to Larry for 34 years. She is engaged in a number of initiatives which benefit home educators in the UK, drawing on her personal experience of educating her own seven children, running groups, activities and conferences, as well as her background in social work. She is a director at Streams (a website dedicated to encouraging, equipping and connecting home educators across the nation), founder and co-ordinator of the Learn Free Conference, and actively works with others to protect the rights of parents in the UK to educate their own children. Juliet's idea of fun is creating, crafting and singing with her barbershop chorus.

## Anne Laure Jackson (BSc OT, Advanced practitioner, PGDip Sensory Integration)

Anne Laure is a home-educating mum of twenty years, whose husband has MS and a visual impairment. As an occupational therapist with post-graduate qualifications in sensory integration, she founded and runs an international business/ministry through which she helps those with OT and sensory issues within their families. She has a passion for helping those with differences or difficulties thrive in everyday life, especially in home education, and her wisdom and compassion have made a huge difference in many families with additional challenges.

## Kirsteen McLeod (BSc)

Kirsteen McLeod is an experienced home educator of over 15 years. She has raised her three children as a lone parent. Two of her children have an Autism diagnosis with associated learning challenges. She lives in rural Perthshire with her emerging young adults and the family dog. When not home-educating, Kirsteen works for Scripture Union Scotland and also helps out at her local food bank. She is passionate about grace, compassion, social justice and Autism awareness. She also likes coffee shops and art.

## Afia Bayayi (BSc Psychology and Sociology, PGCE)

Afia Bayayi is of Ghanaian heritage, navigating the world of home education in her country of birth, the UK, with her Zimbabwean husband of 16 years. Afia married at the young age of 18 and entered into the world of business full-time in 2017. She did this in order to facilitate home education whilst wanting to own her own time and be able to work around her children. Prior to running her businesses, Afia was a qualified teacher for eight years. Her specialism was in GCSE and A Level Social Sciences. Being passionate about her job led her to become Head of Department by the age of 24. Nonetheless, she felt strongly about wanting to invest her time and skills into her own children as a priority, which led to her decision to home-educate. Together with her husband, Afia has three children aged 4, 6 and 8 and intends to home-educate them until they reach Sixth Form.

## Matt Harris (PGDip Youth Work and Community Development)

Matt is a former youth worker who, in 2018, became a stay-at-home, home-educating dad to his two daughters whilst his wife, Nicola, studied at Trinity College, Bristol. Matt's passion is to see people live to their full potential and 'be all they can be'. His strengths are his adaptability, empathy, positivity, love of learning and ability to help people develop. When Matt isn't home-educating, you'll find him trying to keep fit, cooking, listening to a podcast, or working out how to get Wilson and Robin, the family dogs, to behave.

## Siân Lowe (BA Hons, PGCE)

Siân is a former secondary schoolteacher who is now in her third year home-educating her three daughters. Moving her children from mainstream education to home education has been life-changing, life-enhancing and quite possibly the bravest thing she has ever done! Her desire is to empower and encourage those who wish to explore home education for themselves. Siân gets very excited about all that she is learning along with her daughters, and when she isn't furthering her own education, she enjoys nothing more than sitting in a café with a good friend. Siân, along with three other home-educating friends, is a director for Streams, a website dedicated to encouraging, equipping and connecting home educators across the nation.

**Philippa Nicholson**

Philippa Nicholson is a second-generation home educator. The eldest of nine siblings, she enjoyed being home-educated so much that it seemed completely natural for her and her husband, Andy, to choose this route of education for their own children. They are blessed with two girls, Unity and Talitha, and two boys, Ezri and Breeze. Philippa spends the majority of her days facilitating the education of the children. She is also involved with her local Christian home education group, volunteers on the Mothers At Home Matter committee and spends any leftover time reading as many books as possible. Her family live in Essex and are part of a small local church which meets in their home.

**Catherine Shelton (Certified Integrative Nutrition Health Coach; MA (Oxon) in Maths & Philosophy; BA (Hons) in Biblical & Cross-Cultural Studies; PGCE)**

Catherine Shelton is a proud mum of four amazing children and has been home-educating for over eleven years. As a wife of a talented linguist, she and her family lived for many years in a remote village in southern Russia, which is where they stumbled across the joys of home education. When they returned to the UK, they decided to continue home educating because of its many benefits. Catherine is also a Faith-based, Integrative Nutrition Health Coach and a member of the UK Health Coaches Association. She's passionate about helping busy Christian women suffering with stress and fatigue to regain their energy, balance and joy so that they can show up as their best selves and flourish in a life they love once more. Find out more about Catherine on her website at *www.catherineshelton.net*.

**Alberta Stevens (BA Hons Politics & Marketing, MA Christian Leadership-current)**

Alberta Stevens is a British Christian single home-educating parent of Sierra Leonean heritage. She combines home educating her two boys with writing, speaking, podcasting and coaching other home educating parents at Homegrown Sonshine, a home education consultancy which founded during the pandemic in 2020. Alberta specialises in creating wholesome and culturally diverse learning resources aimed at equipping home educators to craft their unique home learning journeys with confidence and ease. Prior to becoming a home educator, Alberta juggled motherhood with helping corporate businesses create social value and impact by partnering with local charities. Before this, she held an 18-year career designing and leading informal learning and leadership programmes in the Middle East and the UK. Fuelled by her current studies in theology and her ongoing interest in spiritual formation and the slow rhythms of Charlotte Mason's educational philosophy, Alberta is devoted to helping home ed parents grow by cultivating rich spiritual and inner lives which she believes inevitably overflows into every facet of theirs and their children's lives. Find out more about Alberta at *www.homegrownsonshine.co.uk.*

## Randall & Mary Hardy

Randall and Mary Hardy began their married life in Manchester, and have lived in Shropshire since 2007. They have six adult children, plus grandchildren at every age and stage. Their first encounter with alternative education was through a small Christian school which operated as a parents' cooperative. Their older children's education took place in this context until they moved on to sixth form college. It was through the school that Randall and Mary heard about home education, which was the route they chose for their younger children, often working in partnership with other Christian families. They maintain a ongoing interest in home education, having witnessed its benefits for various members of their own family. Some of Randall's material may be found on his blog No Nationalisation of our Kids.

# *Bibliography*

Andreola, K, 2018. *Mother Culture: For a Happy Home School.* Charlotte Mason Research & Supply, Maryland.

Arment, A, 2019. *The Call of the Wild and Free: A New Way to Homeschool.* Harper Collins, New York.

Axis, 2021. Available at: http://www.axis.org (accessed: 21 October 2021).

Baker, J, 1964. *Children in Chancery.* Hutchinson, London.

Baldwin Dancy, R, 1989. *You Are Your Child's First Teacher: What Parents Can Do With and For Their Children from Birth to Age Six.* Hawthorn Press, Stroud. 3rd revised edition, 2006.

Bogart, J, 2019. *The Brave Learner: Finding Everyday Magic in Homeschool.* Penguin Random House, New York.

Bonhoeffer, D, 1937. *The Cost of Discipleship.* SCM Press, London, 1959.

Byrne, LG, 2013. *Replenish: Experience Radiant Calm and True Vitality in Your Everyday Life.* Hill Top Press, Indianapolis.

Clarkson, S & Clarkson, C, 1994. *Educating the Wholehearted Child.* Apologia Educational Ministries, North Carolina. Revised edition, 2011.

Clarkson, S, 2020. *Awakening Wonder: Opening Your Child's Heart to the Beauty of Learning.* Bethany House, Minnesota.

Dreher, R, 2020. *Live Not by Lies: A Manual for Christian Dissidents.* Sentinel, New York.

Gatto, JT, 1991. *Dumbing Us Down: The Hidden Curriculum of Compulsory Schooling.* New Society Publishers, Gabriola.

Glass, K, 2019. *In Vital Harmony: Charlotte Mason and the Natural Laws of Education.* Independently published.

Holt, J, 1967. *How Children Learn.* Pitman Publishing Corporation, New York.

Holt, J and Farenga, P, 2021. *Teach Your Own: The John Holt Book of Homeschooling.* Da Capo Press, Massachusetts.

Hood, M, 1994. *The Relaxed Home School: A Family Production.* Archers.

Levison, 2000. *A Charlotte Mason Education: A Home Schooling How-To Manual.* Champion Press Ltd, Ontario.

Louv, R, 2013. *Last Child in the Woods: Saving our Children from Nature-Deficit Disorder.* Atlantic Books Ltd, London.

Macaulay Schaeffer, S, 1984. *For the Children's Sake: Foundations of Education for Home and School.* Crossway Books, Illinois, 2009.

Mackenzie, S, 2014. *Taking a Birds' Eye View.* Available at: https://readaloudrevival.com/taking-birds-eye-view/. (Accessed 18 October 2021).

Mackenzie, S, 2015. *Teaching from Rest: A Homeschooler's Guide to Unshakeable Peace.* Classical Academic Press, Philadelphia.

# BIBLIOGRAPHY

Mackenzie, S, 2018. *The Read-Aloud Family: Making Meaningful and Lasting Connections with Your Kids.* Zondervan, Michigan.

Mason, CM, 1886. *Home Education Series, Volume 1: Home Education.* Living Book Press, 2017.

Mason, CM, 1904. *Home Education Series, Volume 3: School Education.* Living Book Press, 2017.

Mason, CM, 1906. *Home Education Series, Volume 6: A Philosophy of Education.* Living Book Press, 2017.

McTaggart, J, 2003. *From the Teacher's Desk.* BookLocker Inc.

Payne, KJ, 2009. *Simplicity Parenting: Using the Extraordinary Power of Less to Raise Calmer, Happier and More Secure Kids.* Ballantine Books, New York.

Rose, L (Ed), 2016. *What Are They Teaching the Children?* Wilberforce Publications, London.

Stoppard, T, 2014. *Shipwreck. The Coast of Utopia, Part 2.* Faber & Faber, London.

The Children's Society, 2020. *Good Childhood Report 2020.* Available at: https://www.childrenssociety.org.uk/sites/default/files/2020-11/Good-Childhood-Report-2020.pdf. (Accessed 19 October 2021).

Watchman, N, 2006. *Journeying Towards the Spiritual: A Digest of the Spiritual Man in 42 Lessons*, Christian Fellowship Publishers, Virginia.

Yates, J, 2021. *Fractured: Why Our Societies Are Coming Apart and How to Put Them Back Together Again.* Harper Collins, Manchester.